William Sharp

The Human Inheritance, The New Hope, Motherhood

William Sharp

The Human Inheritance, The New Hope, Motherhood

ISBN/EAN: 9783337086480

Printed in Europe, USA, Canada, Australia, Japan

Cover: Foto ©ninafisch / pixelio.de

More available books at **www.hansebooks.com**

THE

INHER

NEW H

HERH

BY

LONDON:

ELLIOT STOCK, 62, PATERNOSTER ROW.

1882.

Dedicated

IN

LOVE AND UPLOOKING

TO MY FRIEND

JOHN ALEX. ELDER.

SINCE THE ABOVE WAS WRITTEN HE TO WHOM IT WAS ADDRESSED DIED SUDDENLY IN HIS ~~————————~~ YEAR. BUT I LET IT STAND AS IT IS. A TRUER FRIEND AND NOBLER SPIRIT NO MAN COULD KNOW.

 To E. A. S.

—

As into some waste space in a dark sky
  A new star swims serene, and calm, and bright,
  A never-fading steadfast lamp set high
    To fill with its immaculate far light
    The lonely darkness of the lonely night—

So swam upon my dark the star of love.
  Before, afar off only had I seen
Like planets in a distant heaven move :
  But when this rebirth of my soul had been,
  It was as tho' Life drew aside her screen ;

The music of the great seas deeper grew,
  A larger message fill'd each echoing shore,
The swaying forests had a meaning new,
  And the sweet songs of birds so loved of yore
  Were sweeter still, and with a lovelier lore.

Life, that once lay like some mere narrow sea
  Between fair promontories and shining sands,
Thence stretched an ocean vast and great and free
  Love was the arc that rose in shining bands
  And join'd the near with far imagin'd lands.

Thou hast been as the light unto mine eyes,
  As music in the strange revolving days:
Around us is the glory that ne'er dies—
  The glory of the sun's awakening blaze,
  The splendour of the moon in cloud-girt ways—

These die not, but they ever bloom and fade;
  The beauty of thy soul is still the same:
A glory for the æons they were made;
  For all eternity thy spirit came
  Straight from thy God in an enduring flame.

O best belov'd,—too dear for faltering words
  To tell thee truly—would that I could sing
With the unconscious rapture of the birds
  That, mated, ev'ry morn till noontide fling
  Their overflowing music thro' the spring:

Or that with deep and solemn measured speech
  Such as the ocean in a windless night
Moans incommunicably to the beach
  That dumbly listens thro' the moon-glare white,
  My words could track thy soul's still tender height.

Thou art my moon, and I thy tide to roll
  Thro' storm and tempest as thro' winds that sleep,
Thy love my pilot is,—I fear no shoal
  Or perilous straits that hidden dangers keep,
  Since thou art with me on the troubled deep.

CONTENTS

—:o:—

" I will make the poems of materials, for I think they are to be
the most spiritual poems ;
And I will make the poems of the ~~" my "~~ body and of
mortality,
For I think I shall then supply myself with the poems of
soul, and of immortality."

WALT. WHITMAN, *Chants Democratic*,
" Starting from Palmanok."

THE HUMAN INHERITANCE.

Visions of life these are/wherein are seen
Types of the human, rounded differently
By age and clime and diverse circumstance.

Childhood, when the child is as a flower
Of wilding growth, and when it is at one
With nature, fellow with the winds and birds.

Youth, when adventure is the salt of life,
And all the passions hot, and when the years
Seem weary if not shifting with swift change.

Manhood and Womanhood, together twined
In spirit, and with equal upward gaze :
Moving with love through toil-ennobled years,
And ever reaching unto higher things.

And Old Age,—work and toil being past : and soft
The memories of sorrows : with the hope
That, after one dark hour, youth comes again !

Types of inheritors of that high life
Which is of all the possible heritage ;
Types none the less tho' few there are who reach
The half-guessed affluence of their periods.

CYCLE I.

CHILDHOOD'S INHERITANCE.

I.

ENEATH the blue vault of a summer sky,
Where little clouds with white wings
    strove to fly
Far from the burning noon, leagues long there lay
Wide heather moors that stretched till far away
Northward faint hills arose and southward rolled
The ocean gleaming with sun-litten gold.

II.

And 'mid a great swell of the purple waste
Close to the sea, a rock, which no hand placed
Thus lonely and afar but which was hurled
A meteor from some ruin'd starry world,
Rose dark and frowning, with its hoar sides scarred
By winter tempests and the fiercely hard

Gripe of the death-frosts that from northland heights
Steal silent through grim January nights,
And traced with furrows by the many tears
Of rainy autumns' thro unnumber'd years.

III.

The purple moorland waste alone stretched wide
Beneath the sun—no thing was seen beside
To break the long still sweep that met the sky,
No mounds of rocks confusedly piled high,
No single tree with clear boughs limned in black
Against the blue, no white and dusty track,
But only miles and miles and miles that swept
Purple to where the leagueless waters leapt.
The old rock stood forth like an ancient throne
Great tho' forgotten, where the winds alone
Paid homage, fair in the shunsine of the day,
Solemn by night with phosphorescent grey.

IV.

Around, the honey-laden bees humm'd loud
With summer gladness ; in a mazy cloud
Whirling the grey gnats rose and wheeled and spun
Swift golden motes within the golden sun ;

And bright with all their royal emblazonries
Flashed like swift darts of fire great dragonflies.
Away across the glowing moors there rang
The lapwing's wild complaint, and far off sang
Hidden in blue a small rejoicing lark
Singing against some unseen yearn'd for mark :
About the heath the yellowhammer's cry
Piped sweet and clear, and often suddenly,
With joyous chirps and jerks, the stonechat flew
From spray to spray, and, darting flame-like through
The scented heather spires to where beneath
The ants had silent kingdoms in the heath,
The green-grey black-eyed lizard flashing shot
So swift the hawk on poised wings saw it not.

V.

O'er all the deep skies arch'd, a wondrous space
Of ardent azure while the sun had place,
That changed to dark deep depths when twilight grey
Dreamt into night, dark'ning to one vast shade
Of purple black, when lamplike star by star
Sparkled or shone or pulsing flamed afar.
Silence save for each blent and natural sound
Of earth and air—where sea-caves made the ground,

By tidal waves of ages undermined,   .
Groan as in travail —when the trumpet wind
All uncheck'd blew—or swelled the incessant cries
Of tossed waves in their breaking agonies.

VI.

Upon the summit of the ancient stone
(Whose birth was in Time's youth), and all alone,
Sat silent, tranced, and motionless a child
Like some sweet flow'r chance nurtured in the wild,
Sat watching seabirds, with his eager eyes
Full of the deep blue of the vaulted skies.
A child, for he indeed was little more ;
A child at heart, such as whom make the door
Of heaven seem open'd here—to whom the seas
Breaking in foam, and scattered spray-swept trees
With long arms wrestling, and the winds on wings
Invisible were wondrous living things.

VII.

A flower, for his wind-kissed locks unshorn
Shone yellow as gold daffodils at morn ;
His eyes were blue as in the golden grain
Windflow'rs are blue, and soft as after rain

Violets that under dripping leaves have lain,
And tender as a dappled fawn's that yearn
For pity when the shrew-mice from the fern
Shake down the dew-drops ; 'neath his sunlit hair,
As early morning, his sweet face was fair
Beneath the sun-brown,—as a white bud rose
That flushes faintly while the June sun glows.
And even as he gazed there deeper grew
Within his eyes a holier softer blue,
Where some thought brooded in their sacred shade ;
It seemed almost as if some song were laid
Asleep upon his face that yet would find
Some perfect utterance for the echoing wind
To carry to the birds ; in reverie
Raptured he saw what these could never see.

VIII.

Oh blessèd time, when all God's world is fair
And to the soul not foreign ! When the bare
Wide cruel wastes of death-encumber'd sea
Seem as the voice of God that thunderingly
Beats round the recreant earth ; when morning seems
The revelation of one's utmost dreams
Of beauty ; when the slow death of the day

Makes all the west one glorious crimson way
For happy souls that die ; and when the moon,
Wheeling her radiant orb thro' the dark noon
Of night, with conscious splendour makes the seas
Unutterably solemn, and great trees
Lost in the shadow stand forth with huge limbs
Ghastly and clear ; when bird songs are all hymns
Of joy and praise, and every wilding flower
Is known and loved ; and when each pent up hour
Seems worse than wasted to the eager heart,
That fain would hear the thrush-wings strike apart
The beech leaves in short flight ere full and clear
Burst the sweet tide of song, or watch the deer
Stand with great eyes amid the fern, or high
Hearken the cuckoo's music fill the sky.

IX.

He seemed content just silently to sit
And watch the breaking waves, the swallows flit
Like arrows through the air, save when along
The summer wind swept bearing the sweet song
Of happy larks, or the repeated cries
Of plovers when they caught the hawk's keen eyes
Fixt on their young—and then he seem'd to be

All sight and ear, as yearning tearfully
To beat with spirit pinions that fine air ˙
Where at the gates of heaven exceeding fair
The bird-songs rose and fell like silver tides,
Or else to be as that royal bird that prides
Itself on flinching not before the sun
But stares undaunted, so he might have spun
Downward with death upon the fierce pois'd hawk,
Saving the moorland brood : not man or boy
Seem'd he so much as some incarnate joy
At one with all things fair, flow'r o' the sod
And insect to the Loveliness call'd God.

X.

As a red rose that in full bloom doth spread
Her soft flushed bosom to the wind ere dead
'Mid fallen leaves her queenliness is gone,
So the fair westering day in glory shone
Heedless of coming night though night was nigh.
The sunset burned afar ; the holy sky
Seem'd filled with heavenly shades mail'd in clear
      gold
Guiding their purple rafts through seas that rolled
Immeasurably far off in crimson fire.

The sea lay tranced watching the day expire,
And tired waves rose and fell as though each pray'r
Of rest long sought were granted.   Everywhere
God's blessing brooded.   And at last the day,
With one long earthward smile, dissolved away
Veiling her head in twilight robes where through,
The palpitating stars shone faint and few.

XI.

From out the darkening vault where they had hid
Through sweltering heats of noon, swiftly there slid.
Star after star, each swimming from the near
Dark blue of heaven as from a windless mere
Rise in calm morning twilights white and clear
Young lily buds that open golden eyes
Which joy makes wider when the day doth rise.

XII.

Far inland, with an oft-repeated cry
The curlew wailed, and swelled mysteriously.
Hoarse sounds from the dim sea.   The boy's face
    grew
White in the dusky shade as swiftly flew
A great ~~white~~ gull close by him, like a ghost

Haunting the desolate margins of the coast :
Great moths came out, with myriad sharded wings
Huge beetles droned, and other twilight things
Hummed their dim lives away, and through the air,
The flittermice wheeled whistling : while the glare
Of summer lightnings flashing furtively
Blazed for a moment o'er the sleeping sea.

XIII.

At last, with a long sigh, he turn'd and slid
From the old rock, and for a little hid
His face amongst the heather-spires that shook
With cool sweet dews : then one last lingering look
Across the twilight seas, where o'er the moon
Within her crescent shallop would sail soon,
When with swift steps he turn'd and westward fled
Across the moor by a little path that led,
Almost unseen save known, till suddenly,
Screened from the vision of the neighbouring sea ,
Low in a dip between two moorland mounds
A cottage lay ; whereto with rapid bounds
He sped, and, bearing with him odours of salt foam,
Entered the little doorway of his home.

XIV.

Almost alone they lived, father and son ;
The elder had come here, life's joy being done
For him for ever, so that at the least
He might have rest.   Nature was his priest
To soothe, and make Hope seem some possible
    thing
And not the gleam of some phantasmal wing.
Deep in his books he lived ; with studious eyes
Scarce noting the young life beside him rise
From childhood into boyhood.   Under skies
Far south his wife was born, and there she bore
The fruit that slew her ; there for evermore
The man's heart yearnéd with a deathless need,
And thus the child grew up like some wild weed
Fair but untrain'd ; a being that loved the birds
And knew their speech, and heard mysterious words
Whispered amid the silence of dim caves
By surging tides ; who loved the winds and waves
With passionate joy ; and whose clear soul was filled
All day with music, as a lyre is thrilled
By every breath of air : night, morning, noon,
The fires of sunset, th' ever changing moon,

The stars, the seas, the moors, the wave-worn rocks,
The ultimate depths of heav'n, the white flocks
Of drifting clouds about the skirts of day—
All these seem'd his in some divine strange way,
And he at one with them, and his glad soul
But one small chord in the harmonic whole.

CYCLE II.

YOUTH'S INHERITANCE.

I.

VAST deep dome wherein the shining fires
Of space hung panting, as though keen
desires
Burn'd in them to spring forth from the blind force
That held them as in leash ; a comet's course
Blazed in the east, and constellations flamed
As through the night they strode ; the famed
Canopus, whom on Syrian wastes afar
Men once had worshipp'd, and the fiery star
Aldebaran, and, sword-girt, great Orion
Whose light feared not the moon's—all these outshone
With splendour from dark heaven, and many more
Which mariners know well when drifting o'er
The far south seas: the Southern Cross agleam
With fire shone high, and, as in some fierce dream
A tigress pants, the pulsing star men know

As Sirius, in ever changing glow,
Blood-red, and purple, green, and blue, and white,
Flamed on the swarthy bosom of the night.

II.

As though the Power that made the Nautilus
A living glory on the perilous
Wild seas to roam, had from the utmost deep
Call'd a vast flawless pearl from out its deep   *s ℓ*
And carved it crescentwise, exceeding fair,—
So seem'd the crescent moon that thro' the air
With motionless motion glided from the west,
And sailing onward ever seem'd at rest.

III.

Below, the wide waste of the ocean lay.
League upon league of moonled waters, spray
And foam and salt sea-send ; a world of sea
By strong winds buffeted. And furtively
At times a shadow loomed above the waves
Only to fade ,as men say out of graves
Troop spirits who flee back at mortal gaze／   *;／*
This shadow was a ship, which many days
Ago had pass'd the doleful straits where sleep ·

The storms that rage and ravin on the deep.
She seem'd a bird, black, with tremendous wings
Poised high above her, a condor-bird that brings
Death in her sweep.   Slowly the shadow grew
Distinct, and the stars seem'd more faint or few,
And the waves waxed wan and leaden, and afar
I' the east the night seem'd troubled : ev'ry spar
Stood forth in outline, and above the topmost sail
The delicate glory of the moon grew pale.

IV.

The night rose from the east, and with slow sweep,
Her shadowy robes about her, o'er the deep
Far westward floated ; the dusk, her sister fair,
With soft remembering eyes and twilight hair,
From out the brooding depths of heaven stole,
And linger'd with her faint sweet aureole
Of trembling light, as though she could not leave
The shadowy ways she haunted, where waves heave
As sighing in sleep, and as a dream the wind
Breathes hushfully.   But lo, the east behind
Quivers, and afar the horizon thrills
One moment, and a seabird wails and shrills
Then sinks to rest again.   And like a dream

That fades as we awake, or like the gleam
Upon a child's face ere it falls to sleep,
The tender twilight faded o'er the deep.

V.

Again the whole east trembled, and a hush
Fill'd sky and sea ; and then a rosy flush
Stole upward, as sweet and delicately fair
As pink wild roses in the April air.
And suddenly some shafts of gold were hurled
Right up into the sky, and o'er the world
A molten flood seem'd imminent, till swift
The rose veil parted in a mighty rift,
And the great sun sprang forth, and o'er the sea
Rose up resplendent, shining gloriously.

VI.

White shone the wind-fill'd sails of the tall ship
Escaping from the waves, fain to outstrip
This giant of the deep : a league behind
The white track she had made danced in the wind
Foaming and surging, while white clouds of spray
Swept from the bows that cleft their wind-urged way.

C

VII.

And suddenly a shout came from the crew,
For one had spied emerging from the blue
What seem'd a delicate pale purple band
Of morning cloud ; no larger than a hand
It lay asleep upon th' horizon line
And like some lovely amethyst did shine.
But this was land, and eager eyes were bent
To take the wonder in.   Even then a scent
Of something sweeter than the salt sea-breeze
Seem'd in the air, odours of spicy trees
And sweet green grass, and fruits, and flow'rs the eye
Sees only 'neath the hot Pacific sky ;
And every heart was glad, for each felt free
For one day from the ever present sea.

VIII.

But after noon had passed with scorching rays
The wind grew slack and ceased, and then a haze
Crept from the quivering north, and to and fro
Wandered the windless waves, as white sheep go
Straggling about the meadow-lands when far
The shepherd strays ; and from the distant bar,

White in both calm and tempest, that enwound
What now was seen an island, came the sound
Of breaking billows in a muffled roar,
As in a shell one hears a wave-washed shore.
And soon the sea itself grew still and mild
And seem'd to sleep, just as a little child
After its boisterous play and fretful rest
Lays down its head upon its mother's breast,
And, smiling, becomes one of God's pure things
Once more; and as with folded wings
An angel sleeps upon the buoyant air
So wholly slept the wind ; while, with her hair
A misty veil about her, Silence rose
And cast o'er sea and sky her hush'd repose.

IX.

As a dream slowly onward drifts to sleep
So stealthily the windless ship did creep
Closer and closer to the foaming bar ;
Noon burned above, like furnace vast afar
Flaming unseen ; and, with a dazzling glare,
The sleeping ocean heaved her bosom bare
As some great woman of the giant days
Supine 'mid mountain-grasses in the rays

Of an intolerable sun might breathe
With panting breasts : far in cool depths beneath
'Mid swaying loveliness of ocean weed
Bright fish swam to and fro, and with fell speed
The pale shark gleamed and vanish'd, as when Death
Is seen a moment 'mid life's failing breath.

X.

At last a boat put off from the ship's side
Urged by swift oars,—a speck upon the wide
And dazzling waste : and soon the bar was crossed,
And the long ridge, where foam for ever tossed
Like fountain sprays around, once past, a mile
Of motionless loveliness without the smile
Of even one young rippling wave stretched on
Till its blue lips the white sands fawned upon.

XI.

Swift in the rowlocks swept the oars, and fast
The boat fled strained and throbbing until past
The azure mile, and on the shelving beach
Its brown keel glided sharply ; each to each
Shouted with joyous cries and boyish mirth
To feel beneath their feet the steadfast earth

Again, to see the scared birds scream and fly
Circling around, the waving palms on high
Heavy with milk-filled nuts, and branches bent
With juicy fruits, and a little stream that sent
Delicious thrills of thirst thro' each one there
So clear it seem'd and like some living thing
Dancing and splashing in its wandering :
And then to feel the very air fill'd full
Of scents delicious stealing from the cool
Green forest shades, heavy magnolias fair
O'er brimm'd with odours sweet, green maiden-hair
Quivering above the intoxicating bliss
Of heavy laden lilies, each a kiss
Lost to the world of lovers, but grown here
To shape and hue, of festooned orchids made
Of colours such as burn in rainbows, fade
Gloriously in sundown western skies,
Or shine within the splendour of sunrise :
Great fragrant blossoms twined amongst the trees
Like prisoned birds-of-paradise, by bees
And gorgeous insects haunted : and such deeps
Of billowy green (the loveliness that sweeps
The soul more swift to joy than brightest flow'rs),
As though the forest were a myriad bow'rs,
Too fair for man, wrought hither into one

For the fair dreams of old who 'neath the sun
Laugh'd in the vales of Tempe, or outrun
The stag in Attic woods, or danced upon
Hymettus and the slopes of Helicon.

XII.

But one amongst the joyous men withdrew
And wander'd inland, for his spirit knew
That rapt delight in its own subtle mood
When the soul craves and yearns for solitude
Akin to its own loneliness of joy.
A man in strength and stature, yet a boy
In years and heart, to whom the whole sweet, fair,
And beautiful world was a thing laid bare
By God for man to love, to whom it seemed
A loveliness more sweet than he had dreamed
Of woman in the passionate dreams of youth :
He saw the joy and glory, not the ruth
And death and grief that unto older eyes
Dwell likewise there, as water underlies
The still white beauty of the frost : but to
The poet it must seem so ever, new
And fresh and wonderful and sweet and true
And ever-changing, for although he knew

The strange coincidence of natural woe
With what to him is as the breath of God,
He sees beyond and deeper—every clod
Of earth that holds a flow'r-root is to him
The casement of a miracle ; in the grim
Reflux, decay, that doth pervade all things,
He sees not but the shadow of death's wings,
But only mists of sleep and change that drift
Till the bowed face of Life again shall lift.

XIII.

As the hot day swooned into afternoon
Hotter and hotter grew the air, and soon
All the north-western space of sky became
Heavy, metallic, where the heat did flame
In quivering bronze ; and the sea grew changed
Tho' moveless still, as though dark rivers ranged
Purple and green and black throughout its deeps ;
At times, as a shudder comes o'er one who sleeps
And dreams of something evil, swiftly flew
Across its face a chill that changed the blue
To a sheet of beaten silver ; then again
It slept on as before but as in pain.

XIV.

And suddenly the ship's gun fired, and then
Three times the ensign dipped ; startled, the men
A moment stared, then down the shingly strand
Sped swiftly, and from the silvery sand
That edged the wave-line launched their boat and
    sprang
Each to his place, and soon there sharply rang
Through the electric air the cleaving oars
That swept them seaward from the island shores.

XV.

The sea seemed changed to oil, heavy and dark
And smooth, with frequently a blotch-like mark
Or stain, as though the lifeless waves had died
Of some disease and lain and putrified.
And like a drop of oil, heavy and thick,
A raindrop fell making a sheeny flick
That glitter'd strangely ; then another came,
Another, and another, till a flame
Of pale wan light flicker'd above the waves
That slept, or lifeless lay, as over graves
New-made a ghastly glimmer drifts and gleams,

Or as that vagrant fire that faintly streams
O'er lonely marsh lands thro' each swarthy night.
· There was a strange, weird, calm, unearthly light
Shifting about the sky, as o'er the face
Of one who had been fair a smile might chase
The horror of some madness half away.
The raindrops ceas'd : from the boat's oars the
    spray
Fell heavily : and then once more it rained
Slow drops awhile the boat's crew gained
The ship, where all with waiting anxious eyes
Watched the metallic gloom of brazen skies.

XVI.

And suddenly there crashed a dreadful peal
Right overhead—the whole world seem'd to reel
And stagger with the blow : the heaven's womb
Opened and brought forth flame : an awful gloom
Stretched like a pall and shrouded up the sun :
Then once again the thunder seem'd to stun
The shaking firmament, and livid jags
Of lightning tore the cloud-pall into rags,
Again and yet again as tho' 'twere hurled
Straight down for the destruction of the world,

And yet again like hell's fire uncontrolled :
And ceaselessly the deafening thunder rolled
Above and all around, as though the ship
Was in the hollow of God's hand, whose grip
Would close ere long and into powder grind.
At last burst forth the fury of the wind
Imprison'd long, which like a wild beast sprang
Upon the panting sea and howling swang
Its great frame to and fro, and yelled and tore
Its heaving breast, tossing thick foam like gore
In savage glee about ; and like a spray
Of blossom whirled before a gale, away
The ship was swept o'er boiling seas that fled
Before the wild wind howling as it sped
Far from its thunderous caverns overhead.

XVII.

And not till then it suddenly was known
That on the island whence their barque had flown
One who had ~~went with them~~ _thither gone_ was left behind—
He who had wandered inland : but the wind
Blew ever with a shrill and doleful cry,
Calling the bloodhound waves to faster fly
And seize the fleeing ship ; a million deaths

Leagues behind follow'd them with clamorous
    breaths ;
To turn were to perish, and so they sped
Onward, as helpless as a whirling grain
Of sand upon a tempest-stricken plain.

XVIII.

Meanwhile the island trembled 'neath the pow'r
Of the rushing wind, as though its final hour
Had come upon it ; but he whose eager eyes
Watched the frail ship being hurl'd far out of sight
Feared not so much himself the tempest's might
But rather for those friends swept far away.
If saved, he knew that some immediate day
Would see the white sails gleaming on the sea
Beyond the bar again, and joyously
He laughed to think of happy hours to spend
Yet here awhile. Two hours passed, and the end
O' the storm came ; and while he watched it sweep
Like a destroying angel o'er the deep
Far to the south, the sun shone forth again,
The birds shook from their wings the clinging rain
And thrilled the air with gladness, and the land
Bloomed out afresh, and on the shining sand

The waves broke with a soft repentant motion ;
Miles and miles stretched the foaming dancing ocean,
Tossing blue waves in glee and whirling spray
Hither and thither, until tired of play
And wearying for calm dreams it also grew
Quiet and still and slept in one dense blue.

XIX.

It was now late in the sweet afternoon,
The hours of shadow and sweet rest : and soon
The day would fall asleep in sunset clouds
And twilight steal and cover earth with shrouds
Of morning dusk, until the solemn night
Would eastward come crown'd with the lambent light
Of the full golden moon.   But still the sun
Hung high in the west, nor would his course be run
For one hour yet or more, and land and sea
Owned him yet lord in regnant majesty.

XX.

On the north-west of the island rose a height,
Crown'd with tall waving palms of coral white
Heaved through long years from sea-depths far below.
Thither the young man turn'd his steps to go

To see the farewell splendours of the day
All marshall'd in magnificent array.

XXI.

He passed whole brakes of sweet magnolias, fair
Orchids with flushed white breasts and streaming
    hair,
Lilies with languorous golden eyes, and flow/rs
That stooped to kiss him from their leafy bow/rs
Hid in green spaces ; then right through a glade
Of trembling tree-ferns wander'd ; then the shade
Of lofty palms enclosed him, till he came
Once more on orchids, each one as a flame,
Scarlet, or white, or purple, tree-ferns high
Warming their trailing tresses 'neath the sky
Where the sun burn'd low down, frond laid on frond
Of spiked green cacti, and at last, beyond
A stretch of dazzling sand, laughing in glee
The blue bright jubilant waters of the sea.

XXII.

And suddenly he started as though stung
By some hid snake, then down his frame he flung
And looked with eager eyes. Upon the strand

He saw brown figures move—a joyous band
Of laughing girls : and lo, upon the crown
Of a great billow that came thundering down,
One fair girl-shape with long hair blown behind
Poised for a moment!   The soft western wind
Thrill'd with sweet echoed cries, and then once more
A great curved billow swooped upon the shore
Bearing an agile form that gleam'd forth bright
Like shining bronze against the sunset light.   ❋

XXIII.

Quite close upon the shore he lay ; so near,
He saw the happy light within their clear
Dark eyes, and saw their joyous laughter make
A sweetness round their lips, and saw them shake
The thick black tresses of their hair, all wet
With salt sea-spray.   He thought that he had met
The fabled syrens, or the nymphs of old
Whom Pan loved dearly, by hard fate compell'd
To leave their antique Greece—and as he stood
Wrapt in the pleasant vision of this mood,
A cry shrill'd suddenly along the sand,
And in a moment almost the bare strand
Stretched white and lonely, for as shadows flee

*a very vivid and beautiful description of
the Pacific Islanders in this native pack
in this volume by Mr. C. W. Stoddard in
"Cruising in the South Seas". (1874.)*

When the sun springs impetuously
From mountain peak to peak so swiftly fled
The nude bronze figures. The sinking sun, red
Like a wounded warrior king, lay down
I' the west to die, taking his shining crown
Of gold from off his brow, which unseen hands
Held poised above him in mid air : the lands
That he had conquer'd thro' the long fierce day,
And seas that owned his rule, faded away
Before his filming eyes, but, ere the night
Should come, once more he rais'd his stricken sight
From out the purple royal robes that wound
About his limbs—stared straight, as on a hound
Baying a lion far off, on light whose size
Gigantic loomed i' the east—strove yet to rise
But could not—so lay back with glaring eyes
Upon the blood-stain'd clouds—while overhead
A star leaped forth knowing his lord was dead.

XXIV.

But he had heard that in these happy isles
Friendly the natives were—that welcome smiles
Met each who wander'd there—so forth he went
Across the shingly strand, then stopped and sent

A shrill cry through the air.   And speedily
Tall lissom figures drew anear ; then he
By signs related how the changeful sea
Had brought him thither, and how hunger made
Him weary : and thereafter, when he stayed
His signs and waited, one who seem'd a chief
Stepped forth and handed him a palm-tree leaf
In sign of friendship, and with kindly eyes
Lifted his hand and waved it all around
As though to say that all things he had found
Were his, that here he might find welcome rest
And live with them partaking of their best.

XXV.

They led him then across the sands to where,
In a delicious hollow where cool air
That late had wander'd on the thirsty seas
Dwelt in green spaces, 'neath great branchéd trees
Cluster'd their huts : and entering into one
The old chief led him as an honour'd son,
And soon sweet fruits and flesh of fowl and kid
Were laid before him, plantain-bread amid
Its broad green leaves, and the strong native wine
The palm-nuts give, and sweet fish from the brine

~~Cluster'd their huts : and entering into one~~
~~The old chief led him as an honour'd son,~~
~~And soon sweet fruits and flesh of fowl and kid~~
~~Were laid before him, plantain bread amid~~
~~Its broad green leaves, and the strong native wine~~
~~The palm nuts give, and sweet fish from the brine~~
New caught, and water from a running stream
That gurgled near like music in a dream.

XXVI.

The ~~sky~~ and tender twilight had now fled,
And all night's starry hosts shone overhead
In myriad fires, and rising suddenly
The orb'd and yellow moon above the sea
Shone full : it might have been the risen soul
From a dead sea whose waves had' ceased to roll.

XXVII.

And at the sound of laughter on the sands
Those in the hut came forth : clapping his hands
The old chief made some summons, and anear
One drew—a living loveliness, with clear
Dark wonderful large eyes whose depths contain'ed
The passionate spirit in the flesh enchained :

D

A mouth like some wild rose bud red, a bare
Bronzed beautiful neck, round which her waving hair
Swayed like the wind-blown tendrils of a vine,
Or like the tangled sea-weed in the brine
Tide drifted to and fro ; her bosom swelled
Urged by her panting heart, as when beheld
Of old the queen, whose face made all the world
One war, the eyes of Anthony—or as
When Helen flush'd when Paris first did pass
Before her with fixt gaze ; around her waist
A girdle of fair feathers interlaced
With cowrie shells drooped slant-wise to her knee,
And small and delicate feet, like those that flee
Among the shadowy hills at dawn when far
The twilight hours speed 'fore the morning star,
Press'd but scarce marked the sand : she stood as one
Tranced in a vision, and he as on that sun
Columbus stared that offered him the West.
Love's fire was litten sudden in each breast.

XXVIII.

Ah ! in the years to come how that night seemed
Some beautiful vision that he long since dreamed !
The moon rose slowly o'er the sea, as though

She linger'd in those heavenly ways where thro'
The stars shone as bright flow'rs : the leagueless deep
Had lullabied its waters into sleep,
And only at long intervals there blew
A cool soft fanning wind that ere long grew
Aweary also, and so stirred aside
The slow reluctant leaves and like a tide
Crept ever farther in amongst the trees
Till in a little dell, with flow'rs the bees
· Haunted all day, it sank to restful ease.
Laughter and wild strange music from curv'd shell
And palm-tree flute far echoed ; the sea swell
Urged hushfully its endless monotone—
And he the ship had left stood there alone
And knew it not, for his whole life was filled
With the utter peace, and his spirit thrilled
With imminent joy, and all his heart was hot
With new-born love, and all else was forgot.

XXIX.

When he that night lay sleeping on his bed
Woven of palm-tree fibre, strange dreams fled
Like ghosts through the dark valley of his sleep.
He dreamt he saw the green weeds of the deep

Swaying unconscious of the light of day,
And 'neath their convolutions lo ! there lay
Two shining gems that seem'd alive with light :
And then he dreamt that dark eternal night
Brooded for-ever, without change, around—
Till suddenly two stars leaped with a bound
From out the womb of chaos, staring straight
Upon him : and next he dreamed that fate
Had wash'd his wan drown'd body to the strand
Where the waves wanton'd with him, when a hand
He saw not pulled him from the brine that made
His tangled hair like sea-weed, softly laid
His wave-tossed head upon a bank of flow'rs, and
    drew
A palm branch 'twixt him and the burning blue
Of heaven ; and then he oped his weary eyes
And met the gaze of one from Paradise :
And then he woke, and knew the gems he saw
Down in the ocean depths with such strange awe,
And the two stars that made th' eternal night
Pregnant with message, and the orbs that o'er
Him bent when death had washed him to the shore,
Were each time but the eyes of her whose gaze
Had flashed to his soul's utmost depths, whose face
Seem'd burned and printed on his heart, whose grace

Haunted his inward vision as when floats
The fair mirage 'fore him who far off notes
Its unsubstantial beauty, shining clear
Yet never to be reached or be brought near.

xxx.

Six days passed, and it seem'd as though he had
Dwelt there since birth : joyous, unthinking, glad,
He was at one with those who lived around.
They called him by some sweet name like a sound
Of distant music, and the name that meant
So much to him and all the quick blood sent
Up to her face when e'er to her he spake
Was Aluhà. Oft by a little lake
That inland lay half hidden by great white
And scented lilies, curtain'd from the light
By tall and shadowy fronds of fern, they strolled
Hand claspt in hand ; and when the fragrant gold
That was the heart of some great forest-flow'r
Fell on their face and hands in a sudden show'r,
Stirred by some quivering wing of bird the heat
Kept silent 'midst the leaves, her laughter sweet
Rippled like falling water, till their eyes
Of a sudden met, and a swift flush did rise

And make her face a ruddy damask rose,
And his hand trembled as of one who knows
A perilous abyss beside him yawn.
And in the tender beauty of the dawn
Together they went down and watched the sea
With little wavelets splashing hushfully
Beyond the breaking rollers, till afar
The east was seen to tremble, and a star
Made of pure gold to twinkle on a wave,
Till suddenly the sun, as from a grave
A soul might spring rejoicing, sprang sheer up
Above the sky-line—and as from a cup
O'er-brimm'd the flooded water pours, clear gold
Along the lifted waves resistless rolled.

                    XXXI.

And on the seventh day the tropic sun
Grew fiercer still ; the noon-heats seemed to stun
Both sea and land, and the long afternoon
Lay like a furnace on the deep : the moon
Sailed through the breathless sky at last and brought
Cool shadows ; till a little breeze long sought
Wander'd on vagrant wings unto the isle.
Where the strand crescent curv'd, almost a mile

From the palm-shaded huts, there was a bend
Of forest, sweet with heavy scents, the end
Of a magnolia brake ; and overhead
Tall tree-ferns waved, and thick grass made a bed
Where the dark sky and stars were seen alone,
And the sea was not save for its hush'd moan.

XXXII.

And there the lovers lay silent and still.
At times the listless wind would send a thrill
Through the dark leaves, or a hidden bird would
    shake
Its wings while dreaming, or a wave would break
On the unseen sea with an unusual sound,
Or suddenly a beetle on the ground
Would clang its sharded wings, ~~but~~ these but made
The silence deeper. Lost within the shade
The lovers lay : her dark eyes watched a star.
Straining in heaven as though its fires impelled
It forth to spring where it far down beheld
The earth in soft light spin ; he watched her eyes
Reflect the panting star-fire in the skies ;
And then he trembled, and once strove to speak
But could not. Then against his flushing cheek

A tress of hair wind-lifted from her breast
Brushed gently : then he sudden stooped and pressed
His lips to hers, and clasped her close and cried
In a strange voice *Aluhà !*   Side by side
Silent they lay awhíle, as though half dazed
By extreme passion : till at last she raised
Her eyes to his with one long look that thrilled
His spirit with love's ecstasy fulfilled.

XXXIII.

And like a dream the long night drifted past,
As a thick mist, stirred by no mountain blast
But moving in some strange mysterious way,
Drifts o'er the steep hill sides.   Faint, wan, and grey
The far east grew, and in the dusky sky
The moon sail'd lustreless, and mistily
The planets shone, and paled each starry fire
Each like some sad and unfulfill'd desire.

XXXIV.

And when the sun rose it was in a mist
Wrought of pale gold, purple, and amethyst,
Changing to lovely carmine, then to rose,
Then to a faint blue haze of heat ; like snows

That melt away before the soft south wind
Each wandering cloud faded the sun behind :
And over all the quivering sky there spread
A deepening haze, so that overhead
The sun tho' flaming fiercely was not seen.
Ere this the light stirred through their leafy screen
And woke the lovers : in his eyes the fire
Of passion was not quenched, and still desire
Dwelt in the shadowy depths of those he loved :
Still hand in hand they lay ; and neither moved,
As though they feared the breaking of some charm
Too dear for speech.   At last she stole her arm
Around his neck and put her lips to his
And wedded him again with one long kiss—
And all the blood within him was like wine
Burning his veins ; his spirit felt divine
In the first flush of love surpassing sweet,
And in this climax life seem'd made complete.

XXXV.

Then hand in hand, with ever and again
Eyes seeking eyes, as though with hungry pain
Love starved for reassurance, ever new
And wonderful,—they went, shaping the dew

That glistened on each leaflet to the ground.
There was an ominous absence of all sound
Such as most mornings knew; the quivering haze
Curtain'd the well-lov'd sky, and to their gaze
It seemed the palms and heavy flowers stooped
Already heavy, and in the shadow drooped
The birds with half closed wings, or swiftly sped
Voiceless to deeper shade : but overhead
A whirling insect flew with a fierce drone
Shrill and metallic : with a stifled moan
The brooding sea remembered some old grief.
And when upon the ground a wither'd leaf
Fell rustling, though not a breath of wind blew
     there,
It whirled in circles thro' the electric air.

XXXVI.

Aluhà passed into her hut, and he
Sought coolness in his own : noon heavily
Drew near, and with a brooding sense of pain
Fill'd up the day.   All nature seem'd to strain
Expectant of some evil, as men wait
Helpless the heavy hand of imminent fate.

XXXVII.

And suddenly like some far distant gun
A long low rumble mutter'd : the red sun
Shrunk thro' a livid mist, and shone no more.
A billowy swell swept swiftly on the shore
Though no wind blew ; the oily sea was freaked
With lines such as a stagnant pool is streaked ;
And the tall palm-trees shiver'd, as a breath
Of icy air had whispered them of death.

XXXVIII.

Again, like far artillery in the sky,
The distant thunder rattled : a low sigh
Moan'd o'er the deep, but not a drop of rain
Fell from above,—then all was still again.
Dark and more dark it grew, as though the day
Were shadow'd in eclipse ; but far away
Strange sudden lights were darting through the
    clouds,
Like gleaming corpse lights o'er the dead sun's
    shrouds ;
And darker still it grew, till overhead
A terrible livid blackness was outspread

And the storm brooded right above the isle.
Still the same awful silence! Mile on mile
Of wan and purply waters lay as tho'
They sank from some fierce scourge, and to and fro
A surface-current twisted like a black
And sinuous serpent; the salt/sea-wrack
Oozed out a filthy scum that sullenly
Blotched the dead calm with spots like leprosy.

XXXIX.

And suddenly, as 'twere the crash of doom,
Heaven seem'd to rock! From out the blasted
    womb
Of the thick darkness belched a stream of fire
Blazing and burning, as though hell's desire
Furrowed the world, that shook and quaked and
    reeled
As deafening by the dreadful thunder peeled
From horrible abysses in the sky.
And in the midst thereof a piercing cry
Of human pain followed a livid flash
Of lightning, when again a dreadful crash
Blasted the air o'erhead while rock and steep
Shook as by motion of the swaying deep.

XL.

Then, as though all the floods that heav'n had stored
For days and days were loose, the dense rain poured
Downward in blinding torrents : till an hour
Dragged slowly past ; and then it seem'd the power
O' the storm had vanish'd. Far off in the east
The thunder howled still, like a savage beast
Famished and tearing at its stricken prey.
But from the isle it was now far away,
And the sun shone once more, and a cool breeze
Blew from the south, and the drench'd dripping trees
Flashed as though clad in shining coats of mail.
And lo I upon the west sea-marge a sail
Hover'd like some white bird,—but heeding not
The sea or what it held the lover sought
His bride of one sweet night, and drawing near
Called *Aluhà!* And then with sudden fear
He saw her father's hut was torn half down
And part all scarred and scorched ; its crown
Of palm leaves was no more, but on the ground
Lay strewn and broken ; and not a single sound
Bless'd his strained ear. With shaking hands he drew
The fallen leaves aside, and then he knew

Whose dreadful cry it was that shook the air
Above the din!   With all her lovely hair
Strewn o'er the delicate bosom's dusky grey,
And with closed eyes, hence loveless, quiet she lay.
Only adown the tender brow there ran
A narrow furrow.   Close by lay a man,
Her brother, with a scorch'd and blacken'd cheek,
And on his face the unenfranchised shriek
Which swift death intercepted : without stain
Or mark dead also the old chief!   All pain
Was over for them, and their little life
Was ended as a dream or bygone strife.

XLI.

So still they lay : he could not quite believe
Each spark of life had fled.   Could cruel fate weave
Such sorrow from her loom for no good end?
But when he took the hand which used to send
Such tremors through him, kissing it again
And yet again, and felt the dreadful pain
Of no response, and in a numbed strange daze
Looked in the eyes where from his eager gaze
Death shrouded up the soul, he knew at last
All that had come to him : his sweet dream past,

His passionate love a thing that was no more
But only a stinging memory to brood o'er,
Life turned a little wearier, and the morn
Of youth grief-clouded, older grown, forlorn—
When all this came upon him the sobs shook
His strong young frame.   And then once more he
    took
His dear love in his arms, and kissed her lips
As though her spirit yet from the eclipse
Wherein it lay might wake, calling her wife
And darling, his dear love, his life,
Till the sobs choked his utterance and stayed
The agony of his loss.   And then he laid
Her gently down, and one long farewell gazed
Then left and wander'd forth as one half dazed.

XLII.

'Twas late in the afternoon when down the strand
He saw one running towards him with his hand
Pointing out seaward o'er the curving bay.
And lo, before his eyes his own ship lay
With yards squared round, and urged by splashing
    oars
The longboat steering for the island shores.

XLIII.

A few short hours ago he would have bid
The old life glad good-bye, choosing amid
The island folk to dwell—but now the land
Was hateful to him, for no loving hand
Would beckon him again by the little lake
That slumber'd lily-clad ; no eyes would make
His heart beat fast with joy ; and never again
Would the dear voice replace the last hour's pain.

XLIV.

So, when the boat's keel grided on the shore,
And eager shipmates clasped his hand once more,
A great weight was uplifted from his heart :
Yet was he loth when the hour came to part
With those who loved him and made him seem
One of themselves.   But soon 'twas all a dream
Strange and unreal, when, standing on the deck,
He saw the island lessen to a speck
In the fast gathering twilight.   Soon his eyes
No more beheld the earthly paradise
Where he had tasted the sweet joy of love,
Yet the same solemn moon that sailed above

Had seen their passion bloom, a tropic flower,
Through one delicious, lost, remember'd hour.

XLV.,

For youth is but a glad forgetfulness,
Or rather, passing onward : the years bless
With such sweet copious gifts, the soul stays not
To linger with sad sorrows best forgot/
But like the tender south wind of the spring
It goes from flow'r to flow'r, while glad birds sing
And the blue skies are fair : what good to wait
By this or that blown rose until too late
To find the sombre autumn drawing nigh
Wherein few roses bloom ?   For steadily
The years come round wherein past youth doth seem
The irrevocable beauty of a dream.

CYCLE III.

MANHOOD AND WOMANHOOD'S INHERITANCE.

I.

 "FIVE years have passed, and still the world has brought
But little change to me.   High things I sought
For mind and hand to do : the world seem'd fair
Before me,. and I felt the strength to dare
And conquer.   Five short years since that day
When, for the last time, I looked on the grey
Belovëd college walls, and knew at last
That manhood had begun and youth was past."

II.

So to himself spake Arnold Selwyn, as
With slow enjoying steps he trod the grass
Fresh with cool dews and gentle summer show'rs
In the sweet dawn of a May day, whose hours

Were sacred here as on the hills and leas
Far from the city smoke—for 'neath the trees
Heavy with myriad lamp-like chestnut blooms
Of Kensington he wander'd : from hot rooms
He came, where all the summer evening through
The dancers had not flagged.   The blackbirds
        flew
About his path, with mellow voices clear
Full fluted, and, from an old beech-tree near,
A song-thrush, poised upon a branch wind sway'd,
Sang wild with its own music, till afraid
With extreme bliss its tremulous thrills piped low
And with a far-off sadness, like the flow
Of windless waters on an alien beach—
Till the soft lights among the green leaves, each
A little waving wing, its heart away
Swept in a tide of joy once more ; the spray
Shook with its wild delight, which thrill'd and
        thrill'd
Till silenced in sheer ecstasy.   It fill'd
The heart of him who listen'd with a glad
Rebirth of youth—such joy as Chaucer had
(A singer like the birds) when wandering
Through woods at dawn in some old English spring.

III.

And the rooks wheeled up black against the sky
Cawing with busy clamour; shrill and high
A distant lark rejoiced; the redbreasts sang
Amidst the chestnut-snows and sparrows sprang
From bough to bough low twittering; from tall
And sunlit limes, in soft aerial fall
The delicate scented blossoms waver'd down,
And sweet the tender grass smelt.   From the town
A distant murmuring sound subdued and far
Hummed thro' the leafy boughs, but did not mar
The woodland sweetness—as we often hear,
Lying 'mid the mossy roots of some old peer
Amongst his fellow oaks, with nought else round
But waving ferns and nestled near the ground
Shy primrose tufts, a low, faint, soothing sound
Steal from some unseen hollow wherein moves
O'er pebbly channels and thro' time-worn grooves
With soft, slow, gurgling music a clear stream
Twisting and turning like a silver gleam.

IV.

But with the gladness was a mingled pain
That stayed the longer: and sad thoughts again

Linger'd like guests unwelcome in his brain.
Though fickle moods seemed with him, moods that
　ranged
From sadness into brightness, for there changed
Often upon his face for a little while
The wearied look for a remembering smile
Of something pleasant—wordless memories
That brought a shining softness to his eyes.

V.

" Five years ago I thought the world lay wide
Before my youth, and that the first spring-tide
Would bear me on to fortune.　As then, still
The world is—but the world is oped by *will*
And not by hope.　And when I lightly drew
My anchor from the old tried faiths, I knew
But little of the yawning depths that roll
With dreadful power around the labouring soul
That seeks but finds no haven.　All seem'd straight
And easy to o'ercome, and fortunate fate
To be assured : too fortunate, alas !
For each of these five useless periods was
To me a snare, and with each month therein
I dallied, thinking I might haste and win

The work that makes true manhood noble when
My spirit should say *now !* Thus was it then,
And so it is even yet. Drifted about
By this view or by that, each put to rout
By every phase successive—with no aim
Of definite purpose, yet desiring fame
In whatsoever thing I undertook
I might have guessed that failure would outlook
My path all round. And yet I know that I
Have gifts beyond the accomplishments that lie
Within the grasp of most ; art/as to me
Been ever a fair dream : it now shall be
Something beyond the pleasure of an hour.
Let me work out my manhood thus, with pow'r
Such as I have, and give to it my heart
And soul : for true laborious work's the part
And portion of each man, and he who shirks
Labour of hand and mind, and feebly lurks
In weary and empty byeways of his life
Moves ever backward. For in steadfast strife
And upward toil alone can there be found
That which each soul to fuller life shall round."

VI.

Hark, the wild thrush notes once again!   He heard
The full soul singing right o'erhead, and stirred
No further step, but listen'd with rapt ears
And thrilling sense : even as in old years
Long past the young Marsyas might have stood
And hearken'd such an one fill all the wood
With matchless music, learning thence the song
Of fluted notes he would regret ere long.

VII.

It ceased, song being at last expressionless,
And onward Arnold went, with on his face
The sunshine of some inner pleasantness.
His thoughts had backward flown to where last night
From out the throng of dancers on his sight
One face had fixt itself, passing him by
Unconscious,—as a dream mysteriously
Bears sometimes from the haunted lands of sleep
A wonderful vision with dark and deep
Presageful eyes, and face that doth inherit
All man's lost dreams of beauty, pale brows lit
As by some inner radiance, and a mouth

Wreath'd with such lips as hers who in the South
Long since Troy razed and wasted for a kiss—
Swims from the depths of sleep, but ere the bliss
Groweth real fades silently away
As into night melts twilight wan and grey,
So that the soul but faint remembrance has
When morning comes.   Beneath him on the grass
He saw the upturn'd face and the deep eyes
Wherein love brooded half awake : the skies,
Smiling on summer with a languid peace,
Held it within their depths ; and 'mid the trees
Shadowed by waving boughs, he saw it move
And vanish—a will-o'-the-wisp of love.

VIII.

And ever and again within his mind
The hours of the past night relived—the wind
Singing an undertone wherein the word
" Lilian " rose and fell, as the sea is stirred
By tidal heaves at ninth-wave intervals.
He stood within the flashing mirror'd walls
And watched the dancers pass, until that face
Glanced close to his with its supreme sweet grace
Of loveliness—and then as one whose eyes

Watch the long purple line of land arise
Out of the seas after a weary time
Of tossing to and fro in a bitter clime,
So kept his gaze transfix'd where'er she went.
At last the time came when his head he bent
Before her, and heard spoken the sweet name
That now the wind repeated. A soft shame
Flushed the pale delicate face, as a white rose
Were crimsoning beneath the kiss of June,
Being conscious of his furtive eyes ; and soon
They left the crowded rooms, and in a cool
Green-leaved recess, where/in a little pool
Fern-fringed and rock-girt, with a gentle sway
Of sound a sheeny fountain splashed alway,
They sat unseen of any. Something strange
Had come to him ; he knew not what, some change
That brought a thrilling sense of a delight
Of imminent revealment, while the night
Seemed some prolonged enchantment leading on
To joys expectant afar off. Upon
His ears the blent strains of the music fell
With hushful sound, and o'er his soul a spell
Seemed cast, sweet as on fields of asphodel
Shadowed by palms of Paradise doth steep
Each new-come spirit in a joy of sleep.

IX.

They err who say that love must be of slow
And well-proved growth—as if the heart must glow
Alone as the fanned flames of a slow fire.
Love ofttimes springs, clothed with a wild desire,
And takes the reins of life in hand ere quite
The soul hath felt the change; and fills the eyes
With ardent longing and a glad surprise
And a strange light and rapture beyond speech.
One looks upon another, and for each
The past has suddenly grown old, a flame
Is lit within each heart, and a soft shame
Dwells in each look, and life yearns unto life
And all the world with hopes and fears seems rife.

X.

Before they left that night both eyes had told
A similar tale, and each stirred heart did hold
The rumour of a sudden happiness.
But few words passed ; yet love doth oft express
Himself in silence best. The casual touch
Of lace, or falling flow'r, or hand,—all such
Were ministers of love that sent a thrill

Through him, as o'er the brooding surface still
Of a calm sea swift airs go wandering—
And when his lips once said some little thing
And laughed, whereby his breath breathed on her hair
She flushed and trembled, and her bosom fair
Heaved with a quicken'd motion, a swift beat
That whisper'd something new and strange and
    sweet.

XI.

At last they had to part, but when she went
He saw before him still each lineament
Of the fair girlish face ; and but one word
'Mid all the noise around his spirit heard,
The one word " Lilian." And when far away
Her carriage rolled through the awakening day
And chastened sweetness of the dawn the air
Seemed full of music, and the wind to bear
On its soft pinions, as a bird might do,
The burden of his name whose love she knew.

XII.

Hark ! hark ! O sweet and clear, again, again,
The over rapturous thrush with a half pain

And half extremity of joy makes all
The air alive with song : with fluted call
The blackbird sounds his summons to his mate,
And the rooks cawing in the air await
The signal for their uniform ascent
To distant fields.   And homeward Arnold went
With a changed life and purpose of his own
And the long follies of his youth outgrown.

XIII.

Three months passed, wherein life at last was found
No idle dream, but ever steadfast round
Of labour—and where love half-guessed had spun
A weft of magic.   Love indeed had won
His soul from sloth, and given to him a hope
That would not die again, but that would ope
The future to his arms : and love had brought
Each aspiration that he once forgot
Back to his mind once more ; and love each day
Was with him and his soul did sway
Hither and thither/ever tending higher, /
And ever grew the strength of his desire
For her he loved, as a long trammelled fire
In mines beneath the soil doth grow and grow

Until at last the flames flash to and fro
Above the enfringing depths. She was to him
A faith, a hope, a joy, the wine at the brim
Of that which held life's last draught and supreme :
She was the moon to lead his waves—the dream
To inspire—the guide to reach the road—
The hand to slack the burden of life's load.

XIV.

Not yet had words escaped him—yet she knew
He loved her ; and her fair face daily grew
Sweeter with knowing it ; and her heart was fill'd
With joy. And ofttimes bright dreams she would
    build
Wherein the two with wedded love would reach
To that which poets dream of when they teach
Love is the key of life. And so went by
The months, until the clear autumnal sky
Saw the oak change to russet, and the plains
Grow yellow, and the equinoctial rains
Wash the white dust from off the beech-tree leaves,
With heaped up here and there damp amber sheaves
Of elm and chestnut, and the sunburnt mould
Gleaming with fallen leaves of lime-tree gold.

XV.

Both had been absent from the dusty town
Through the late summer. Where the cliffs shelve
    down
Most steeply to the surging Cornish seas
A little village lies, which the spray flees
Right over when a wild wind's from the west—
And there they both by chance had found a rest
From weary London for a time ; but soon
She left again, and then, as is a time
With sudden discord filled, so seem'd the place
To Arnold not the same when once her face
Haunted the shores no more. Yet still he strove
To reach the secret that he sought, and wove
Upon the canvas a fair dream that would
Inherit all the passion of his mood.
So the days passed in work, the nights in dreams
Of love, save when the August moon's full beams
Tempted him forth to hear the night waves chime
Their inarticulate prophecies sublime,
And the sea lay his hoary head beneath
The shadow of the cliffs and faintly breathe.
So went the happy weeks until at last
He knew that he must leave : one night he passed

Wandering along the ever-sounding shores
Rapt in sweet dreams—the next he heard the
hoarse
And constant turmoil of the streets. But here
He was near that which made his life seem dear.

XVI.

Cloudless the sky was, calm and soft and blue :
Cawing, the homeward rooks in circles flew
Above the lofty elms, and everywhere
The sparrows twitter'd thro' the warm still air ;
Eastward the chestnuts, cluster'd near the banks
Of the Long Water in irregular ranks,
Faded into a tender gauzy mist,
And the Pond deepened into amethyst
Bright with the mimic sails that flashed upon
Its rippling wash ; and a faint carillon
Of far-off bells blent with the bleating cries
Of sheep and children's laughter. The flushed skies
Grew crimson with the splendour of the sun
Burning the west, and like a vestal nun
Pure, cold and white the crescent moon hung high
In the mid-heaven, and Venus' flashing eye
Watched from the dove-hued south half tremulously.

XVII.

West of the Serpentine the beeches make
Cool shadowy haunts, wherein whene'er they shake
Their leaflets to the ground, 'tis like green rain
Waving adown from boughs where it has lain
Hid from the scorching sun—so cool and green
They seem a glade far in some woodland scene
Where the birds build and sing and never know
Disturbing fears/with near some streamlet slow
Meandering with cool lisping sounds, where calls
The kingfisher by day, and when dusk falls
The moorhen, nightjar and the whistling bat.
And in the shadow of those beeches sat
Arnold and Lilian, listening without words
To the last twilight cries of drowsy birds,
And watching the flushed glory of the west
Halo the sinking sun that sought his rest
Where none could see him, and the golden flow
Raiment the palace with a tender glow.

XVIII.

And when at last the highest elm-tree branch
Caught the last gold, and the small waves did blanch

Upon the pond into a gloamy grey
And the last crimson cloudlet paled away,
Each turn'd to each, with gaze that was the gate
Where through their soul's speech went, confederate
In desire ; and then his hand took hers, and still
No word was spoken, but an equal thrill
Stirred every nerve of each deliciously.
At last he spoke, saying, " *Lilian*," tenderly,
" Lilian, I love you !"   And beneath the tears
That dimmed her eyes he saw the promised years
Wherewith in love she dower'd him : and life
Seemed changed from night to day, to peace from
    strife ;
And silence lay between them like a sea
Wherein two wandering currents suddenly
Meet and unite and no more separate be.

XIX.

Homeward at length they went when the dusk grew
By stealthy shades to-night.   Each spirit knew
The sundering of self when a soul gives
Its best to another.   The hour that lives
Memorial thro' each life that once has loved
Had come to them ; and as deep pools are moved,

F

Twin depths upon a lone hillside, and stirr'd
By the same wind, so at the sudden word
Of love both hearts throbbed wildly with the same
Divine emotion—thro' each life the flame
Already burn'd that yet a pillar of fire
Would be from out the wastes of low desire
To guide each soul to emprise ever higher.

XXI.

Before the leafless boughs beneath the snow
Dreamed of dead summers or the leaves that low
The winds had scatter'd were grown wholly old
And shrivell'd, and still some lingering gold
Shone palely here and there against the haze
Of rainy skies in bleak November days,
Their lives were joined in one, their streams were blent
In one seagoing river! Forth they went
With hearts strung high and each soul confident.

XXI.

Twin married lives hence hand in hand they chose
Their paths together—fronting whate'er rose
Of evil or of sorrow on their way
With equal gaze: and ever day by day

Their great love deepen'd, as a pine-tree clings
Still closer to the rock o'er which it flings
Its matted shade ~~despite the~~ winds that beat
Its lonely height: and as the flow'rs make sweet
The blessëd days of Spring, that every year
Seem to become more wonderful and dear,
So little joys and hopes made daily life
Seem fair to them, soothing the fret and strife
That is the heritage of all.   Their love
Indeed was life: and dear the joys thereof.
Ah, love is not a seed blown heedlessly
By any devious wind across the sea
That hems us in ; a seed that in earth's womb
Grows till the day when in its perfect bloom
The sun's kiss warms it and its blossoms make
A fragrance for the wind to lift and shake
Along the tufted grass—till one day come
The frosts of winter when the birds are dumb
And the leaves fall'n and dead, when it is blown
Seaward again from whence it once had flown, —
Blown hence by devious winds, rewhirled again
Back to the wastes amid wild wind and rain !
Nay, love is not like this: it is the breath
That blows across the sterile lands of death ;
It is the wind that o'er the tropic seas

Blows ever in a steadfast changeless breeze ;
It is not but a dream that in man's sleep
Dries up a little while tired eyes that weep
Then fades to let the weary day begin,
But is the goal that every life must win
Or suffer.   Love is the immaculate wind
That blows across the drifted years behind
Our human course, and bloweth far away
Beyond the furthest beacons on our way ;
Eternal round our little finite day.

CYCLE IV.

OLD AGE'S INHERITANCE.

I.

NORTHWARD long leagues of plain, until
    the eye
    Grew wearied with a vast monotony
Like that of the far seas, long leagues of plain
Grass-cover'd, which for weeks and months had lain
Beneath the scorching of the Austral sun,
Thirsting with drought : beyond, the sands begun
And stretched a dreary desert where nor beast
Nor man were often seen. Far to the east
Rolled also the long grassy plains, tanned brown
And crisp with heat, where the hot sun shone down
Day after day, with rays athirst to find
Some lingering moisture—where no cooling wind
Blew ever, save when the lamplike stars swung low
From the vast depths of heav'n, and rising slow
The moon usurp'd the night ; then ofttimes blew

A fresh wind steadily, that lately knew
The cool breath of the South Pacific seas.
West of the loghouse, gum and wattle-trees
Rose miles away, and miles beyond them still
Dim densely wooded ranges, hill on hill
Cover'd with mint and box and sassafras,
White stringy bark and the coarse upland grass.
Southward the ground shelved downward to a stream
That lispëd through the rushes like a gleam
Of beaten silver, shallow, yet that filled
The sunken pools where rains of winter spilled
Themselves and were not lost : and overshore
The grassy plains, but greener, swept once more
For half a mile, until like a green sea
They laved against a base whence solemnly
A vast and ancient forest stretched away.
About the house itself, rough-hewn and grey,
A lovely creeper, such as stars the trees
With large and yellow blossoms that each breeze
Casts like gold globes of fragrance o'er the ground,
Clung with a wavy tenderness around
The stain'd peeled logs ; and at one end there grew
An English rose that underneath the blue
Australian sky gave red blooms full as sweet
As the winds kiss in Kent, that loved the heat

Of the long day that on the log walls streamed
For burning hours.   In front dark violets dreamed
Of their ancestral haunts in English woods
Where the thrush flutes his song and the dove broods
Through the green-shadowed noon ; with lilies, white
And holy as the shining stars of night,
Brought also o'er the seas from out the West.
Acacias shaded them, in one a nest
Where a sweet songbird dwelt and wooed its mate
Each spring recurrent with insatiate
Heart of music.   A wide verandah ran
Round half the house, which, whene'er noon began
To burn the freshness up, still kept a place
Wherein cool airs might wander—with the grace
Of vine leaves overgrown, that large and green.
Made a soft, wavy, and delicious screen.

II.

This was the house which, after years gone by
In many wanderings underneath the sky
That held the Austral stars, John Armitage
At length had built for home ; here to old age
His last ten years had grown, and here he knew
That he would look his last upon the blue

Deep skies he loved—not glad to leave the earth
Yet wishing not to shun the soul's rebirth
Trough the dark womb of death.   About him were
His children, flowers around his sepulchre
Of years—and like sweet youngling buds new blown
His children's children, who were yet his own
To love and cherish.   Only she who bore
This noble fruit on earth would never more
Hear each loved voice say *Mother*, or take hold
Of tiny hands, or in her arms enfold
The weary one who slept.   She who had been
His wife and friend thro' every changing scene
Had left him years ago, and in his eyes
The ~~long lone grief remained~~ till Paradise   /silent/
Should one day see the lovers meet again.
But full of peace he was, and the dull pain
Of loss beyond all words lay down so deep
In his soul's depths it almost seemed to sleep.

III.

Life still was full of pleasantness, of peace
And calm content: for when his years should cease
The record would go down of one whose life
Through all the stress and peril of its strife

Still stainless was, of one who bravely faced
The early dangers of an unknown waste
Undaunted through each failure till at last
The years that nothing brought but toil were past.

IV.

The summertide was full, and through the heat
The flowers gave up their heavy odours sweet
In rich comminglement, as fancies go
Wing'd and rich-hued for ever to and fro
Amidst the haunted silences that are
The realms of reverie, where, like a star
Alone in a wan dusk, the soul doth seem
The mystic dreamer or itself the dream.

V.

Since from the wattles, at the break of morn,
The joyous magpie sang its lilting scorn
For those who waken'd not,* till now the noon
Had burned itself away and twilight soon

---

* The Australian magpie is the sweetest songster, though within
limited compass, that one meets with in the Antipodes.

Would be the shadow of a finish'd day,
The old man had been glad, for far away
His flocks and herds were scatter'd o'er the runs
Far stretching, and to each one of his sons
He had apportioned out an equal share,
Feeling the burden of his years a care
Best lighten'd now.   The busy day being done
He rested 'neath his vines, watching the sun
The deep blue of the sky to crimson change
And golden hang o'er the last purple range.

VI.

The heat still made a silence everywhere,
Save when, at intervals, the startled air
Shook with the laughter of the mocking-bird
Strident and harsh : or when afar was heard
Once only the sky lyre-bird's voice from deep
Within the forest, where the stream did sleep.

VII.

And as a dream before him his past life
Moved in a vision—all the toil and strife,
Adventure, love, and sorrow, and death and all
That fate had brought : and heard dead voices call

Like faint sweet echoes from a distant world.
He saw the day on which the sails were furl'd
Upon the ship that lay in port at last,
And how his eager wandering eyes were cast
Upon the new strange land : and how the days
And weeks went by until he sought the ways
That led due north thro' almost trackless bush
Till far from men, and still did onward push
Until before his eyes the unclaimed plains
Lay stretched for leagues, and saw the winter rains
Fill up the lonely stream with floods that would
Outlast the drought.   And how the years went,
    rude
And rough, but happy, often stirred and thrilled
With danger ;—till all things being fulfilled
That he had hoped for, one week he rode down
To the far distant port, already a town
Where he had seen but huts, and to his side
Clasped one he welcomed as his promised bride
Come over seas to join him.   And how sweet
The after years slid by on rapid feet
Joy-wing'd : for ever their love grew and grew
From year to year, unchanging, deep, and true.

VIII.

And how at last a dreadful day there came
When she he loved lay dying, and the flame
Of life slow flicker'd to its certain end..
Above the dear dead face his lips did blend
To take one farewell kiss, and then he rode
Far through the bush to bear alone his load
Of bitter anguish, and to let his tears
Flow for the vanish'd sweetness of his years.

IX.

'Twas the full tide of summer, and the days
Were sated with the cloudless, changeless blaze
Of the fierce sun : but close to a small pool
Of running water, shaded by the cool
O'erarching tree-fern fronds, they made a grave
Lonely and sacred as where sea-depths lave
The coral beds where pale drown'd mariners lie.
The vast primeval forest round—the high
Deep dome above, the wondrous stars at night
And the strange glory of the moon's soft light—
These watched and brooded o'er her grave, and kept
An endless watch above her where she slept.

X.

A lyre-bird sang a low melodious song
Far off, then ceased : a soft wind swept along
The lofty gums and breathless died away :
And Silence woke and knew her dream was day.

XI.

Hush, from the trackless depths comes what sweet
   sound
Ineffable ! Do spirits underground
In hollow caverns ring phantasmal chimes
For elfin deaths in fairy sunless climes—
Or does some sad aerial spirit high
In serene air suspend the listening sky
With sweet remember'd music of joy-bells
Changing for death ? Hush ! how it swells and
   swells ,
Still sweet and low and sad,—as tho' the peal
Were chimed in forest-depths where never steal
Sounds from the world beyond, and where no noise
Breaks ever the long dream. It was the voice
Of the mysterious bird whose bell-like note
Chimes through the Austral noon as church bells float

e/

O'er lonely slopes and pastures far at home :
Sometimes but once it sang, as when the foam
On northern seas sleeps on the ebbing tide
And scarcely stirs the Inchcape's sounding side
To one faint clang : then ceased : then once again
Tolled out with silver sweetness its part pain,
Part reverie over some belovëd thing :   ·
At last it too was still, recovering
Some dream to brood upon with voiceless peace.
To each who listen'd there a calm surcease
Of sorrow came, and in each aching breast
There was a sense of toil foregone, of rest.

XII.

Before him these dead years and joys repassed,
Watching the sun go down.   His thoughts at last
Brooded upon his spirit's imminent flight
From life, when unto him the eclipsing night
Would come with shrouds impenetrably dark.
Yet death he feared not : whether his soul's barque
Should sail the infinite deeps knowing no end,
Or to some far, far strand its course should tend
Whereon at last to rest and voyage no more,
Or whether it should founder ere the shore

Of any goal be seen, he cover'd o'er
For ever by the waves of death,—not less
Would he thank God for the great happiness
Of having lived at all.   Why should man seek
That which his soul might find itself too weak
To bear—God's own supreme eternity?
Shall not the cycles or the aeons be
Enough for him,—his spirit find a goal
At last?   Nay, whether the tried human soul
Lives out new lives on earth again alone,
Or speeds triumphant far beyond the zone
Of that which we call Time till, aeons pass'd,
It finds its ultimate goal and rest at last,
Or whether it eternal is, with Him
Whom we half think we see, our eyes being dim,
It still is well.   In each alone His breath
Would be the Lord of life, the Lord of death.

XIII.

Such were his thoughts this last day of the year
Waning 'mid summer heats instead of clear
Cold skies and frost and icy northern wind.
At last the sun's flames burned right out behind
The furthest range ; a strange delicious blue

Hung o'er the south and west, as spirits drew
Their filmy veils of azure gossamer
Out of the depths of heav'n and trailed them
  where
The great gums spread their branches thro' the air.

XIV.

But ere the short and shadowy twilight came
The bush was no more still : each tree became
Alive with sound, and the cool dusky skies
Shrill with the shrieks of parrots and the cries
Of crested cockatoos and parrakeets
In thousands, swarming from their green retreats,
With over all the hoarse and chuckling sounds
From laughing-birds ; and when with mighty bounds
The kangaroos fled far in sudden fright
There swelled the dingo's howl.   In the cool light
The fierce cicalas whirred their defeaning noise
From ev'ry bole, and oft a querulous voice
Told where opossums hid : with resonant hum
The grey mosquitoes wheeled around each gum
Ceaseless and fierce : and not until had come
The night itself grew all the clamour dumb.

XV.

Slowly the vast round ^ustral moon became .
The glory of the night : and each a flame
Purple, or blue, or white, the stars hung low
From blue-black skies.   Serene, and calm, and
    slow
The last night of the year to death did go.

XVI.

And when the faint flush of the newborn day
Quiver'd above the wan horizon grey
And deepen'd tenderly, the soul of one
Whose years of patient waiting were all done
Greeted with happy gaze the glad New Year
Far hence.   At last he now would meet the dear
Expectant eyes, and feel the longed-for kiss
Once more upon his lips foretell of bliss.

XVII.

The rosy dawn still deepen'd steadily,
Till of a sudden all the eastern sky

G

O'er brimmed with gold : and from a wattle-tree
A magpie sang the new year's jubilee—
High, sweet, and clear the silver music trilled
As though the singer's heart with joy was overfilled.

THE NEW HOPE.

(A VISION OF THE TRAVAIL OF HUMANITY.

G 2

Dedicated anew
to
my friend and fellow-worker
A.M.C.

THE NEW HOPE.

IN these dark days of storm and stress and
    strife
        That wand'ring man, whom some strange
    fate hath curs'd
With blinded vision 'mid the glory of life,—
Where the clear blaze of light should else have burst
Upon him with its splendour from the first,
Cheering his wayward path—still strives to find
Soul's egress from the gath'ring gloom behind :

Still strives, despite strange dreams that chill the soul,
And deadening weight of countless centuries,
And baffled hopes that lead to some false goal,
And mighty yearnings and triumphant cries
Drown'd deep amid unspeakable agonies,
And ages, breaking in a glorious dawn,
Setting 'midst desolation bleak and wan ;

Still strives against the mist of some strange doom
That shrouds the universe to find a way
That, twisting thro' the stars, doth reach the womb
Of all creation, where the omnipotent sway
Of central life with unbeclouded ray
For ever triumphs, and the Hand that wakes
The spheres harmonic perfect music makes.

Dimly he knows an unremember'd past
Wherein he had an unknown birth afar
In those great deeps of time which reach at last
Those utmost years, when earth, a flaming star,
Quiver'd in heaven like a blood-red scar,
And the moon belched her fires, and higher spun
The huge mass of th' intolerable sun.

Deep in the dark abyss of primal years
He shudder'd into life, and groped with hands
Uncertain up creation's gradual tiers
Until a day when sovereign he stands
And knows for his the mighty youthful lands,
And views the seas break with an alien roar,
But laughs and names them his for evermore.

Dimly in vague uncertain dreams he knows

How long unnumber'd centuries have rolled
Above him with their tide of savage woes,
Dim years, whose hoary memories enfold
Strange secrets mortal tongue hath never told—
Beginnings vast, portentous, and sublime
With Titan-struggles towards a fuller time.

And later still, but not less vague, he dreams
Of elder days in the vast Asian plain
Fed by the waters of forgotten streams,
When tribal hordes appeared and gather'd grain
Where only desert sands before had lain ;
Till, growing to mighty hosts, they spread to where,
Southward and westward, new lands seem'd more fair. .

Where in those dim and twilight lands the soul
Woke slowly to the secret of the stars,
Till Godhood shone from midnight pole to pole ;
And in the fiery flash of burning Mars
Prophets beheld God's summons to new wars,
And every circling moon that made the plains
Whiter than snow heard the wild priests' refrains,

Wild songs of warlike worship, and swift prayer
Snatching at hope, and burning sacrifice,

And maidens with their wealth of desert hair
About them floating, in their dream-fill'd eyes
The victim ecstasy when the deep skies
Rang to fanatic tumult, with sweet breath
Chanting the god whose secret name was Death.

When, 'mid the desert cities before dawn
The wild-eyed priests with long rejoicing call
Summon'd the faithful thro' the silent, wan,
Grey, twilight morning to the eastern wall
To wait, till one great moment saw them fall
Prostrate in worship,—and above the sands
The sun-god rose with blessing for all lands.

Dimly man these remembers : scarce less faint
The solemn morning of Egyptian years ;
The long lost glory and the deathless taint
Of lustful Pharaohs, and the countless tears
That fed the Nile from unremember'd biers
Of sun-scorched, whip-lashed slaves, by whose death-
      toil
The slow wise Sphinxes crown'd the barren soil/

To look for aye with superhuman gaze
Across th' inhabitable waste of sand,

And see, mayhap, far off these latter days,—
And, farther still, some mighty moulding Hand
Shape the predestined fate of every land—
And seeing, speak not—only, far off, where
The sands fade wave-like, watch with steadfast stare :

And far removed from all the busy strife
Of populous cities dwelling by the Nile,
How the great pyramids, through human life
Incalculable, 'neath the cold calm smile
Of Ramses, grew, and watch'd mile after mile
Whiten each year with myriad human bones,
And heard whole generations pass in groans.

Faintly afar he hears the throbbing chant
Of worshippers by old forgotten fanes,
Harsh cymbals clashing, and fierce breaths that pant
From dusky maidens madden'd by wild strains—
Tall brown-skinned maidens from the burning plains,
With breasts sun-moulded, and with shadowy eyes
Inheritors of Egypt's mysteries.

Where swart Assyria swelters 'neath the sun
He lists the anguish of the priests of Baal ;
He sees the chamber sacred unto *One*,

Where daily sounds a low ecstatic wail
From maiden beautiful, rapt, naked, pale—
The bride of God—yet yearning with fierce, fire
For mortal love's unsatisfied desire :

As in a dream he sees tumultuous hosts
Spread locust-wise o'er devastated lands,
And swarthy warriors bathe by Red Sea coasts :
He hears the clamour of battle on the sands,
And the swords swing in fierce delirious hands,
And in the purple air sees pennons fly
Scarlet, as dipped in blood of those that die.

Dimly these bygone memories return,
As to the full-grown man the faint far days
Of childhood in his recollection burn
Faint as the glow-worm's lamp on moonlit wall—
A few brief visions cross again his gaze,
But still the silent ages that have been,
Silent remain behind an unpierced screen.

At times his eyes in backward vision strained
Behold more clear the phantoms of the past,
When mighty kings of shadowy memories reigned
And each great teacher's utterance was cast

Like seed abroad—as fruitful seed to last
From scatter'd sowing till maturing days
Found golden-fruited boughs in every place.

His inward-looking eyes thus view once more,
Where in the almond blossom scented air
The white pagodas line each river shore,
A vast assemblage list with wond'ring stare
New solemn accents fall from lips that dare
The wrath of troubled priests,—and the clear
    voice
Confucian call, " No more in dreams rejoice ! "

Like far off swallows, striving rest to gain
In long pursued and ever fleeing spring,
Winging their flight o'er sea and desolate plain
From winter's frown to where glad song-birds sing
All day and night 'mid sweet lands blossoming—
So sped the mighty teacher's word-wing'd thought
Afar beyond where wrangling priests still fought.

For as a runlet bubbling from a hill
Struggles thro' moss and rocky channell'd steeps
Till one day all its waters shiver and thrill
As far below the shining ocean sleeps,

And crown'd with spray with one great cry it leaps
From earth-chain'd life to that maternal breast
Where every seaward river findeth rest :

So wends by slow degrees and tortuous way
New truth's thin streamlet thro' far scattered minds,
Till soon or late there dawns a pregnant day
Borne on the wings of revolution winds,
And the scant streamlet widening leaps and finds
Its waves wash fruitful teeming lands at last
And roll a highway to the ocean vast.

Or, deeper still, he sees that ancient Ind
Where empires grew, religions wax'd and waned
Leaving faint cloudy memories behind,
Till of these also no dim trace remained—
Till, like a wave that gathers waves, there gain'd
The mighty soul of Buddha devotees
From Cashmere snows to distant Cingal seas.

He views some silent windless twilight die
And fade into a sultry moonlit eve :
Above, the purple shaded star-lamped sky—
Beneath, the Ganges, whose swift waters leave
An utter'd echo of old thoughts that grieve—

And, rising o'er the sands that shelve its tide,
Great shadow-haunted palms dream side by side.

Seated thereby, a man with far-off eyes
That pierce the darkness lying beyond death,
Speaks low with fervent words divinely wise—
And, as the final word he uttereth,
The silent audience, like a pent up breath,
Once more are conscious of the earthly air :
They look again, and Buddha is not there —

He hath passed by ; and every conscious star
Leaps in the heavens as if his gaze to meet ;
He passes thro' the jungle, and afar
The tiger growls within his grim retreat,
But stirs not ; the immeasurably sweet
And midnight music of the nightingale
In quivering worship greets him sad and pale.

Godhood is visible to natural things
More clear than to the soul—the woods that dream
Become vast choirs shaking their green-branch'd
    wings
Angelic, and every forest stream
Lifts up its chiming murmurs, and the gleam

That is earth's smile grows more divinely bright,
Burning with fire of spiritual light.

The many colour'd memories that haunt
The long-undwelt-in mansions of man's mind
Point westward now : across the Hellespont
His spirit strives the chain'd past to unbind ;
Palm-shadow'd mystic Ind grows faint behind,
And, rising over the rejoicing sea,
Greece, sun-crown'd, stands—serene, and great, and
    free :

The storied fame of all the old-world hills
Is made apparent : double peak'd Parnassus
Doth skyward dream, the white air slowly fills
With sweet blown scents from off Pentelicus,
And the bees hum in violet-loved Hymettus,
Olympus guards green Tempe, and the dawn
Rests like a band of gold on Helicon.

Clearest he sees the sovereign city rise,
Queenlike and glorious in her ancient state :
The Parthenon, supreme beneath the skies ;
The marble-pillar'd theatre where the great
Thunder of Æschylus bared the vault of Fate ;

And, with a deathless splendour such as his,
The flow'r-like glory of the Acropolis.

As one who dreams, and sees a great fair land
Spread out before him, watching with pleas'd
   eyes
Mountain, and stream, and forest ever fann'd
By exile minstrel winds from the blue skies,
And far seas moaning for lost Paradise
In sad eternal music (for these keep
That deathless secret in their utmost deep)—

Starts suddenly, and sees a face he knows
Grow into light that makes the rest a dream—
So, dreamlike, from man's vision backward flows
The old Greek glory, like a fading beam
O' the moon before the dawn's first amber gleam,—
And, fixt, his concentrated vision sees
The broad brows of the clear-eyed Socrates.

Seated amid great dusky olive shades,
That move reluctant 'neath the breathless trees
Till 'mid wild rose and honeysuckle glades
They hide and dream, and fann'd by the cool breeze
That from the white foam-crested sounding seas

Bloweth with briny odours, he doth rest
And muse on life and death—and which is best.

The great wind of the human spirit blew
Thro' this Greek soul, which organ-like gave birth
To clear majestic notes of music new,
And, from the old compound of sorrow and mirth,
Wrought a new scheme of God, and man, and
    earth :
Through him it blew such mighty harmonies
His voice still sounds adown the centuries.

The weary soul of man finds rest in these,
The lives he lived to in his earliest days,—
Whether his wing'd thought with brave pinions flees
To that far past half lost to human gaze
When the soul of Egypt, weary with men's frays
And blood and anguish, hid with all her lore
In the great Sphinx she stares from evermore—

Or whether, later still (and like the dove
From seas alighting on green olive boughs)
Resting with him whose heart of boundless love
Made all the Orient echo with its vows—
Or circling round the fate-confronting brows

(A swallow finding spring) of him who drank
With cheerful soul the cup of hemlock rank.

These bring him peace, these names awaken hope
But still his spirit knows another name :
A later star this rose upon life's slope,
Later, but fuller ; yet the Syrian's fame
Rose from an unknown birth, a death of shame
Rounded it off—and though he is long dead
His voice still peals like thunder overhead.

Man feels him still, and knows him not a dream
Dreamt in forgotten days—no empty breath
Blown out with unheld meanings, but a stream
As of white light upon black seas of death—
Or as a glad great living voice that saith
The one word *Water*, where 'mid burning sands
Men famish'd yearn with scorched beseeching
    hands.

He still is part man's present. It may be
The unborn years slow forming in Time's womb,
Shall rise and live and fade successively
And know him not, save as a prophet whom
Past ages worshipp'd as the Lord of Doom—

H

A bodiless echo sounding thro' all time
Some meaningless message that was once sublime.

Thus may it be : meanwhile man's spirit is
A wind-harp answering to the Nazarene :
Man is a beach where the sea's mysteries
Are whisper'd low, or thunder'd through a screen
Of white mysterious foam—where God is seen
A waving arm about a dream of eyes :
A fluctuant sea beneath Christ's wind man lies.

The human soul still shudders with the sob
That thrill'd the dusk of drear Gethsemane,
The bitter cry no lapsing years can rob
From sorrow wedded to eternity ;
That garden dreamed a vast futurity,
That weary night, of fierce successive woes—
Of good men's scorn, and pitiless hate of foes.

Man turns with weary gaze and looks again
Into his troubled past : his tired eyes see
A calm shore fringed with dead wind-echoing
        cane,
And tall flags swaying in hushful Galilee ;
A bittern booms his sad call sullenly,

And, with an hourly pain, a plover's cry
Wails like a wailing soul thrust from God's sky :

The yellow moon, half drown'd in deep dark
    blue,
With still remaining crescent curves a trace
Of gold upon the vast profound ; a few
Great stars, heavy with changeful sphere-fires, gaze
To the lake's utmost depths, and in the bays
Seem to lie panting, as when side by side
Great water-lilies move in a moving tide :

One sits on the dim shore as though his sight
Held not familiar things of wave or land ;
His eyes burn slowly with some inner light
Of scarce hid glory, and his listless hand
Traces his central thought upon the sand
Till the scooped grains read *God*, and then
Father, and *Infinite Love*, and *for all men.*

He stirs once at the desolate bittern's boom,
And prays for man : when the wild plover cries,
His heart throbs with the mystery of Doom :
And when the windless twilight water sighs,
The tears grow slowly in his human eyes,—

He sees the scourge, the cross, the hyssop rod,
Death, and the grave—beyond, the glory of God!

Such are the dreams man knows have made his
    life :
And yet, his youth and boyhood past away,
His manhood finds him still at endless strife,
And life unrounded by a fuller day ;
Faiths rise, and live, and flourish, and decay ;
And, as a helmless ship by every wind
Blown here and there, so seems man's baffled
    mind.

His years have seen him oft—as some tired ox
Stops wearily by some delicious rain
Of clear spring water hid by ferns and rocks
From the rough highway dust, and so again
On with long aching miles until its pain
Sinks at some similar fount one glad time more—
Cease from the weary road he travelleth o'er

And rest with such as Buddha, such as Christ ;
Rest with them, live with them, hope with them, be
A sharer in each old joy sacrificed ;
Think with their mighty searching thought, and see

With their clear eyes beyond mortality—
Then suddenly find all things vain, and rise
And stagger forward blind-like 'neath blank skies.

He hath been as a man with toil aweary
Yet mocked by baffling sleep upon his bed,
And sometimes eased with dreams wherein no dreary
Phantoms of hideous days and years stain'd red
Stare ever at him, and no fair hopes dead
Rise ghostlike weeping, and no more in pain
Old aspirations move white lips again.

The fair dream stirs and fades away, as breaks
A soft young cloud before the ruthless wind—
And as the cloud in snowy feathery flakes
Weeps towards the earth for ravish'd life behind,
So the sweet dream dispell'd can no more find
Joy in itself, but melts in bitter tears
And is a dream no more for coming years.

Fair hopes for ever baffled, and the way
Of life as hard to climb !—thus grim Despair
With fixt immoveable lips that never pray
Walks by his side unchidden :—ev'rywhere
The wide world throbs with life, the summer air

Palpitates with the outsung souls of birds,
The milk-time lowing of the sweet-breath'd herds

Sounds from the meadows, from the windless fir
The cushat calls, and somewhere, as a voice
Heard in a dream, the cuckoo's note doth stir
The high-air silence, with a humming noise
The wild bees haunt the clover, and rejoice
The heaven-loving larks half lost to view,
Small founts of song in the still sea of blue,

And sea, and wind, and hill, and flow'r, and grass
Make up with separate music one great choir :
And then Despair says, " Fool, all these things
          pass
To nothingness, as stubble in the fire
Doth wholly burn—and deeper still and higher
The woman *Vanitas* with blank cold eyes
Scans deepest depths and sweeps the utmost skies

" And sees nought there save ever day and night
A faceless shadow move, that with cold hands
Incessantly draws back from the dear light
Some living thing, a bird from forest-lands,
A leaping fish, a lizard on the sands,

A babe from its young mother, and the breath
From a great soul—and this, and man, is Death !"

And at these words man look with tearless eyes
And hearkens with deaf ears : heav'n's song-fill'd
vault
Is loud with discord ; the divine surprise
Of the sun's advent hath some hidden fault ;
The mighty morning winds no more exalt
The wondrous regions that were once their own :
And, knowing this, man answers with a moan.

At times he turns and looks with steadfast gaze
Into the coward eyes of the drear shape
That with him toils the intolerable ways
And all the earth with hopelessness doth drape,—
And then the shadow fades, and swift escape
To all the glory and splendour of the earth
Man makes again—a veritable new birth.

And often now in the great peaceful calm
Of early mornings some faint distant song
He seems to hear—as though an echoed psalm
From heaven adown the gold clouds waved along,
Or distant angel-wings bore up the wrong

And misery of the world to where griefs die
And wake in rapture singing through the sky.

He hears, and young hope stirs within his heart,
A fledgeling bird that dare not rise as yet
On untried wings thro' the chill air to dart :
He cannot quite the bitterness forget
Of all the ended dreams that he hath met
On life's long pilgrimage—thus hardly dares
To hope again as on his way he fares.

But day by day the Christ-dream changing takes
A grander form : no longer in the past
The Saviour dwells—His voice afar off makes
A music deep, as of an organ-blast
Fill'd with harmonious prophesying vast :—
Twin souls divided, seeking each the other,
One calling *God*, and one crying ever *Brother*.

The new Christ leaves the starry fields of heav'n
And through the mist of space seeks still for
    man :
At times some sign immaculate is giv'n,
Then spiritual winds of yearning fan
Earth's mists awhile aside, and God's great plan

Unfolds in part a moment to his view
Then fades again in the sky's signless blue.

Man's soul is as a pine upon a height
Fronting dim seas—at times each branch a lyre
Of morning music, when the golden light
Waves round its boughs with unconsuming fire,
And soft-wing'd winds re·echo the desire
Of each lark's song, and all the world seems fair
With the eyes of summer smiling ev'rywhere :

And later, when the evening mists have crept
Up the steep slopes, it sigheth wearily ;
A slow sound breaks as though each tired wave wept
     wept
A wailing child upon the mother sea ;
A cold wind strikes its chill'd wings suddenly
But doth not take the air ; and some vague woe
Through each strong bough doth with a tremor go :

Then comes the night ; and the tempestuous deep
Lashes the height with spray, and wild winds cry
With dreadful voices—till its branches leap
And beat the air with suppliant agony,
While Death stares down from the deserted sky ;

And somewhere in the darkness seems to grope
A searching voice that moans "*There is no hope !*"

Thus joy, despondency, and deep despair
Alternate with him : yet each new year brings
A growing strength the ways of Fate to bear :
A great hope deepens with successive springs
That somewhere Truth, the highest angel, sings
A great glad song that, hearkening, man shall
   find
His eyes grown clear, and be no longer blind.

One truth, more old than the time-honour'd hills,
More ancient than the hoary ancient sea,
Before the world was, or the sun that fills
The world with day, or in the vast, blank, free
Space of heaven the first star fierily
Burn'd thro' the dark and silence—one great Word
That spake, shall wonderfully again be heard.

Beyond the wheeling atom of the earth,
Beyond the utmost sun that lights this sun,
A vision of life in some divine new birth
Where seed of man and breath of God are one,
And the old blind groping is for ever done—

This breaks upon man's sight—his fret and strife
Sink at this vision'd glory of new life.

Beyond himself, beyond the human soul,
Farther than Christ or Christ's own farthest
  love,
The source of life, that makes the ages roll
To vast sad music till at last they move
Crown'd and triumphant to new birth above,
Dimly man now discerns, with eager eyes
Lit with the light of some divine surprise :

And with the vision, as a tall tree sways
All blossom'd o'er, with mingled love and awe
His whole soul blooms into the flower of praise—
Not for the working of some great cold law,
But that great truth beyond the petty flaw
Of human doubt—that mighty love, whose breath,
Whose gift to life is never-dying death,—

Eternal change, no stagnant blissful dream !
Forth from the life supreme man's spirit went :
He hath gone thro' the darkness till the gleam
Of light at last shines on him well-nigh spent :
Rest shall he have, as earthly sleep is sent,

To make new life more dear ; then onward still
'Neath the clear light of the omnipotent will !

There is no deathless life—but blesséd death
Kisses the soul asleep, that when at last
It wakes again with new triumphant breath
It heeds no more the weary toilsome past :
Thus shall it be until the æons vast
Draw man so nigh to God no human sight
Can farther pierce th' ineffable great light.

Thus, dark and gloom behind, but light before,
Man takes new strength. The lights of past times
    grow
Fainter and fainter, but afar doth soar
A vaster glory—as when from the low
Sea-wash'd horizon with a motion slow
The full moon rises, and each lesser star
Seems by a gentle hand withdrawn afar.

MOTHERHOOD.

MOTHERHOOD.

PART I.

I.

ENEATH the awful full-orb'd moon
  The silent tracts of wild life lay
  Dumb since the fervid heat of noon
. Beat thro' the burning Indian day ;
And still as some far tropic sea
Where no winds murmur, no waves be.

II.

The bended seeded tops alone
  Swayed in the sleepy sultry wind ,
Which came and went with frequent moan
  As though some dying place to find ;
While at sharp intervals there rang
The fierce cicala's piercing clang.

III.

Deep 'mid the rice-field's green-hued gloom
  A tigress lay with birth-throes ta'en ;
Her swaying tail swept o'er her womb
  As if to sweep away the pain

That clutched her by the gold-barred thighs
And shook her throat with snarling cries.

Her white teeth tore the wild-rice stems ;
    And as she moaned her green eyes grew
Lurid like shining baleful gems
    With fires volcanic lighten'd through,
While froth fell from her churning jaws
Upon her skin-drawn gleaming claws.

As in a dream at some strange sound
    The soul doth seem to freeze, so she
Lay fixt like marble on the ground,
    Changed in a moment : suddenly,
A far-off roar of savage might
Boomed through the silent sultry night.

Her eyes grew large and flamed with fire ;
    Her body seemed to feel the sound
And thrill therewith, as thrills a lyre
    When wild wind wakes it with a bound
And sweeps its string-clasp'd soul along
In waves of melancholy song.

VI.

Her eyes grew large and flamed with fire ;
    Her body seemed to feel the sound
And thrill therewith, as thrills a lyre
    When wild wind wakes it with a bound
And sweeps its string-clasp'd soul along
In waves of melancholy song.

VII.

Her answering howl swept back again
    And eddied to her far mate's ear ;
Then once again the travail pain
    Beat at the heart that knew no fear
But some new instinct seem'd to rise
And yearn and wonder in her eyes.

VIII.

Did presage of the coming birth
    Light up her life with mother's-love,
As winds along the morning earth
    Whisper of golden dawn above ?
Or was it but some sweet wild thought
Remember'd vaguely e'er forgot ?

I

IX.

Some sweet wild thought of that still night
  When underneath the low-lying moon,
Vast, awful, in its splendour white—
  Two tigers fought for love's last boon :—
The striped and fire-eyed terrors strove
Through blood and foam to reach her love ?

X.

Of how their fight so deathly still
  Fill'd all her heart with savage glee ;
The lust to love, to slay, to kill,—
  The fierce desire with him to be
Whose fangs all bloody from the fray
Should turn triumphantly away :

XI.

Of how at last with one wild cry
  One gript the other's throat and breath,
And, with hell gleaming thro' each eye
  Shook the wild life to loveless death ;
Then stood with waving tail and ire
Triumphant change to swift desire ?

XII.

But once again the bitter strife
  Of wrestling sinews shook her there ;
And soon a little howling life
  Met her bewildered yearning stare ;
Till, through her pain, the tigress strove
With licking tongue her love to prove.

XIII.

No longer fearless flamed the light
  Of great green eyes straight thro' the gloom,
Each nerve seem'd laden with affright,
  The eyes expectant of some doom ;
The very moonlight's steady glare
Beat hungrily about her lair.

XIV.

A beetle rose, and hummed, and hung
  A moment ere it fled—but great
In face of peril to her young
  The tigress rose supreme in hate
And, with tail switching and lips drawn,
The unreal foe scowled out upon.

XV.

And when a mighty cobra, coiled
  Amid the tangled grass roots near,
Hissed out his hunger, her blood boiled
  With rage that left no room for fear,
Till, with a howl that shook the dark,
She sprang and left him cold and stark.

XVI.

But when a feeble hungry wail
  Smote on her yearning ears she turn'd
With velvet paws and refluent tail
  And eyes that no more flashed and burn'd
But flamed throughout the solemn night
Like lamps of soft sweet yellow light

XVII.

To where her young was ; where she lay
  Silent, and full of some strange love
Long hours.   Along the star-strewn way
  A comet flashed and flamed above,
And where great waste of solemn blue
Spread starless sailed the vast moon through.

XVIII.

No sound disturb'd the tigress, save
   Stray jackals, or some wild boar's pant
Where thickest did the tall rice wave,
   Or trump of distant elephant ;
Or, when these fill'd the night no more,
The tiger's deep tremendous roar.

PART II

I.

VAST, solitary, gloomful, dark,
        Primeval forests swept away
        To where the gum and stringy bark
    Against great granite mountains lay ;
And through their depths the twilight stole
And dusk'd still deeper each dark bole.

II

Deep in their pathless tracts there reared
    A huge white gum, whose giant height
When winds infrequent blew appeared
    To brush the stars out from the night :
A mighty column straight and vast,
Solemn with immemorial past.

III.

And at its base upon a bed
  Of fern-tree leaves strewn o'er the ground
A woman lay as though lying dead—
  Dark, rigid, still, without one sound:
Her fixt eyes lifted not, nor saw
The great stars tremble in strange awe.

IV.

Couch'd near upon the tufted grass
  Two wither'd long-haired women bent
Two dusky bodies. No sign was
  Made ever them between, nor went
From swift, slant, startled eyes a glance
To break the spell of their deep trance.

V.

They crouch'd with heads bent down between
  Thin, black, uprisen knees ; their hair
Hid their dark faces like a screen,
  And, scored with thorns, their feet lay bare :
Hour after hour had watched them so,
Three shadows fixt in sphinx-like woe.

VI.

At times some wand'ring parrot's voice
 Clanged through the dusk ; from dead trees nigh
A locust whirred to deafening noise
 And shrill'd th' opussum's frequent cry ;
And hour by hour some slim snake stole
Hissing from fallen rotting bole.

VII.

At last, above the farthest range,
 The full vast moon sail'd o'er the trees :
The dead-like woman felt some change
 Thrill through her body : from her knees
Each shadowy watcher raised her head,
And stared with eyes of moveless dread.

VIII.

Beyond—within the ghostly shade
 Of immemorial gums aglow
With phosphorescent light that made
 Each trunk burn taper-like,—bent low,
A savage, bearded and long-haired,
Wild eyed across the pale gloom stared :

IX.

And when his shifting restless eyes
  Caught the drawn woman's birth-time pang,
He shrill'd a wild yell to the skies
  And high with tossing arms upsprang,
Beating with eager blows a drum
And shivering with some terror dumb :

X.

The list'ning women once again
  Sudder'd and grew more still with fear—
Not at the harsh drum's maddening strain
  But at the spirits that were near,
The awful souls of hated dead
That creep round each wild travail-bed ;

XI.

The white-eyed sheeted things that steal
  Down dusky ways and lie in wait
And from the shade their death-darts wheel
  And wreak unseen their deathless hate :—
For these the fierce drum clanged and beat
The summons of a swift retreat.

XII.

What strange thoughts wander'd thro' the mind
   Of her who writhed in travail sore?
As, bearing scents and sounds, a wind
   Blows pregnant from some distant shore,
So may have blown some wind of thought
Memorians from a past forgot,

XIII.

Drifting across her yearning eyes
   Stray visions of lost happy days ,
And filling with strange vague surprise
   The dreary sameness of her gaze—
Dim sweet memorial hours long lost,
Scorched by long suns, numbed by long frost.

XIV.

But soon the wafted breaths that blew
   From off the deep drown'd past were blown
Aside before some sharp wind new
   Of sudden agony.   A moan
Shook on her lips, and from her womb
A new life crept to outer gloom.

XV.

The watching women rose and went
  With deft hands unto her : the man
Hush'd his tempestuous instrument,
  And with fleet silent footsteps ran
To where, asleep in moonlight, lay
Some huts rough built from branches stray :

XVI.

And soon thereafter, in the light
  Of the vast moon, the tribe stole out
And fill'd with cries the startled night—
  Till—with claspt hands and one wild shout,
They circled round the riven frame
Of her whose blank eyes knew no shame.

XVII.

But as some feeble strength came back
  She stretched out thin and claw-like hands,
With eyes as one who on a rack
  Yearns for mercy, or on strange lands
Lifts outspread arms towards his own—
So yearn'd she with a mother's moan.

XVIII.

Within her famish'd eyes no more
　The hunger of the body burned,
But on the fruit her womb long bore
　Their light unspeakable was turned :
And all the hunger of her love
Lighten'd the child's eyes from above.

XIX.

Vast, solitary, gloomful, dark,
　Primeval forests swept away
To where the gum and stringy bark
　Against the granite mountains lay :
Till, as the great moon grew more wan,
Stirred the first heart-beats of the dawn.

XX.

And o'er the pathless tracts where reared
　The huge white gum, whose boughs had seen
The woman's birththroes, light appeared
　And lit its leaves with golden green,
And shone upon the straight trunk vast,
Solemn with immemorial past.

PART III.

I.

FAINT scent of lilies filled the room,
    Hush'd in sweet silence and asleep
    Within the dim delicious gloom :
No windy lamp-flame strove to leap
Amidst the moveless shade, but faint
A soft light burned from censer quaint.

II.

And dimly through the gloom loomed large
    A carven bed that seem'd to sail
Like ghost of some great funeral barge
    'Mid shadow seas no men might hail—
Till from its depths suffused with night
    The wan sheet dreamed to gleaming white.

III.

And lo, half hid, like some white flow'r
   Breasting the driven snow, there lay
Expectant of the awful hour
   A waiting girl, who, far away
Beyond where vision reacheth, gazed
With eyes by some strange glory dazed.

IV.

Like two strange dreams they were, wherein
   Played subtle lights of other life,
Deep depths, scarce cognisant of sin,
   Serene, beyond all clamorous strife—
Two seas unsoundable as night
Yet lit with to utmost depths light.

V.

Silent she lay, as one who low
   In some dim vast deserted nave
Bends rapt in mingled love and woe
   While the wild passionate sweeping wave
Of organ music sweeps and rolls,—
The burden of all suffering souls.

VI.

Silent she lay, for as a palm
  Within a thirsty desert feels
A low wind break the deathly calm
  And drinks each rain-drop as it steals
Between its dry parch'd leaves, so she
Felt God's breath fill her fitfully.

VII.

The soft low wind of life divine
  Entered the darkened womb, and there
It cleft the mystic bands that twine
  The folded bud of childhood fair,
Which, as an open'd, lily, fell
From death to life's strange miracle.

VIII.

A perfect bud of human flow'r
  Immaculately sweet and pure,
Shall God's first influence in this hour
  Through all thy coming life endure,
And thou expand to perfect bloom
Untouched by crash of neighbouring doom ?

IX.

Or, O sweet perfect human bud ,
  Shall rains thee dash, and wild winds sweep
Thy fair head to the mire and mud ,
  And, with praying hands, thy mother weep
Such tears of anguish as no pain
Shall ever wring from her again ?

X.

Soft, soft, the wind of life doth breathe :—
  Some angel surely fans the while
The faint new litten spark beneath,
  And prayeth with a piteous smile
That it may live, and living be
A victor 'midst humanity.

XI.

Silent she lay who soon should give
  This life to life : her secret thought
Strove mid the happy pass to live
  Again that day she ne'er forgot,
That day when her young love took wing
From maidenhood's sweet-scented Spring :

XII.

When hand in hand she trod the ways
  Flow'r-strewn with him, and felt his eyes
Turn'd full on her with such deep gaze
  Of love triumphant that the skies
Seem'd but a hollow dome where rang
Sweet tumult, as though angels sang :

XIII.

How the hush'd drowsy afternoon
  Slipt through the summertide, till low
In the dark tranquil east the moon
  Rose vast and yellow, and more slow
The flaming star that lights the west
Lulled the sea-waters to their rest :

XIV.

How in the bridal chamber shone
  No other than the full-moon's light,
And how between the dusk and dawn
  A wind of passion fill'd the night
And bore resistless soul with soul
On to love's utmost crowning goal.

K

XV.

Silent she was, but as her mind
    Made real once more that perfect day
Her body trembled, as a wind
    Had blown upon her where she lay,
And in her eyes serene and deep
Joys unforgotten woke from sleep.

XVI.

As on a mighty midnight sea
    Wind-swept, and lit by a white glare
Where intermittent lightnings flee
    And deafened by the thunderous air
Split up with tumult, one great wave
Doth rise and scorn an ocean-grave,

XVII.

And, gath'ring volume as it rolls,
    Doth sweep triumphant till at last
It thunders up the sounding shoals
    Of stricken promontory aghast,
And leaves its crown of foam where high
The cliffs stare seaward steadily :—

XVIII.

So from love's throbbing pulsing sea
  All lightning-lit by passion, reared
A mighty wave resistlessly
  Of mother-love, which as it neared
Fulfilment broke in one glad cry
Of sweet half-wond'ring ecstasy.

XIX.

Hush! the great sea is still, and low
  The night-wind wanders; hush, for calm
The mother waits the body's woe!
  Silent she lay; mayhap a psalm
Of sacred joy sang deep within
The maiden heart unstained by sin.

XX.

Mayhap the inward vision saw
  The unborn soul arise and stand
Great in a people's love and awe,
  Crown'd not with gold by human hand
But sacred with the bays that wait
The victor in the strife of Fate:

K 2

XXI.

And, deeper still, beheld afar
  The billows of the ages sweep
A mightier soul from star to star—
  So ever upwards thro' the steep
Dim ways of God's unfathom'd will
But aye by fuller periods still.

So shall it be for ever : evermore
The mystic chain of mother-love shall twine
Around the world, and link these three again.

(NOTE.)

THE form of expression I have adopted for these Transcripts (the following being but a portion of a series forming a kind of private *Liber Studiorum*) is founded on the Tuscan *Rispetto*. " This," to quote Mr. J. A. Symonds' definition, " is the name commonly given throughout (Tuscan) Italy to short poems, varying from six to twelve lines, constructed on the principle of the octave stanza. That is to say, the first part of the *rispetto* consists of four or six lines with alternate rhymes, while one or more couplets, called the *ripresa*, complete the poem."

In broadly adopting the *rispetto* as the most fitting means of expression for my purpose, I have made the first part uniformly consist of six octosyllabic lines, not with alternate rhymes but rhyming *a, b, b, a, c, c,* and have detached the *ripresa (d, d)* therefrom, intending it as a rule to be the means of some supplementary touch, heightening the effect by bearing in some way or other upon the broad outline produced in the preceding six lines.

TRANSCRIPTS FROM NATURE.

I. SUNRISE ABOVE BROAD WHEAT-FIELDS.

HE pale tints of the twilight fields
Have turnéd into burnished gold,
For waves of yellow light have rolled
From the open'd east across the wealds ;
While 'mid the wheat spires far behind
Stirs lazily the awaken'd wind.

A skylark high (a song made bird)
Sings as though God his singing heard.

II. THE STONE-BREAKER.

He stoops all bent and bowed and worn
With arm uplifted o'er the stones :   ·
Each stone is as the poor heart's moans,
Each stroke one less to that drear morn
When he too, broken, cast aside,
Shall die with no one by his side.

The ~~gold~~ of the red sun makes all   *glow*
The landscape one fierce lurid pall.

III.   WILD-ROSES.

Against the dim hot summer blue
    Yon wave of white wild-roses lies,
    Watching with listless golden eyes
The green leaves shutting out their view,
The tiny leaves whose motions bright
Are like small wings of emerald light :

White butterflies like snow-flakes fall
And brown bees drone their honey-call.

IV.   LIGHT OF THE SETTING SUN ON
MOUNTAIN-ASH BERRIES.

The flame of the September sun
    Streams backward from its western bed ;
    The countless berries overhead
(Above me where I rest) have won
A crown of glory such as shone
Never upon King, Solomon :

O'er the horizon spreads a flood—
The selfsame hue—some dead god's blood.

V. PINE-WOODS. *(Silence.)*

Tall, dark, majestically stern,
  With something in their solemn mien
  Of awe, some sense in the deep green
Of life-joy never to return ;
Miles east, dark rain-clouds haunt the day—
Miles west, the sea lies cold and grey :

And overhead, suspending flight,
A goshawk hangs in the drear light.

VI. THE WINDMILL. *(Gathering storm.)*

Four huge black arms against the sky—
  Still now, and waiting for the wind ;
  No clouds in the blue night behind,
But faint far storm-mists trailed on high,
And in the east a shadow black
With fringes split like wild sea-wrack :

It moans, and surely moves at last
In travail with the rising blast.

VII. SEA-WRACK.

Across the grey sea-hollowed rocks
 The waves with sleepy motion glide,
 And in the long wash of the tide ·
The sea-wrack's brown and tangled locks
Sway gently as though nevermore
Wild blasts should rage upon the shore :

And now and then between the slim
Long locks the silver fishes swim.

VIII. THE BLUE HERON. *(Solitude.)*

Here sheer into the emerald lake
 On either side the hills slope down,
 In the long darkness of whose frown
Rarely the young lambs dare to make
Their bleating cries ; no sound is heard
Of even any wandering bird :

But standing on a great grey stone
A grey-blue heron broods alone.

IX. SHELLS ON THE SEA-SHORE.

A yellow stretch of rippled sand
  Curved by the bay to two gold lips ;
  Ah look ! the blue sea slyly slips
Faint frothing up the shingly strand—
Just takes the kiss, and then for fear
Reflows, but ebbs to reappear.

The sea-shells strewn around sing low
The secret sea-things that they know.

X. THE NIGHTINGALE.

The curving elm-boles meeting make
  An archway, where the sun at morn
  And, after dusk, the moon's white horn
Seem framed 'mid dark green leaves that shake
In little vagrant puffs of wind
Faint wandering in the wood behind :

Moonlight and darkness now—O hear !
The *jug-jug-jug* divinely clear !

XI. THE SWOLLEN RIVER.

Between the lush low-lying banks
  The swollen river, dark and deep,
  Hath something dreadful in its sweep :
Just here, in melancholy ranks,
The shaking poplars stand and know
Some dim presentiment of woe.

O'erhanging weeds defy the wave,
Roses and lilies find a grave.

XII.   MOONLIGHT AT SEA.

Far eastwards broods a darkness black,
  As black a shadow on the west ;
  But sleeping on the heaving breast
Of midway ocean lies a track
Of glittering, shining, silver light,
A zone miraculously bright :

Hung as a lamp before God's ways
The moon fills mid-space with her blaze.

XIII.   A DEAD CALM AND MIST
(Towards evening.)

The slow heave of the sleeping sea
  With pulse-like motion swells and falls,
  And drowsily a stray gull calls
The very wail of melancholy ;
All day the moveless mist has slept
On the same bosom east winds swept :

No breath of change in the grey mist,
Save just a dream of amethyst.

XIV.   LABOURERS RETURNING HOME.

Across the turnip-fields green-grey
  And ploughed up pastures, furrowed brown,
  Now that the hot fierce sun is down
The weary labourers seek their way—
Down the rough road with sun-baked ruts
To yonder dismal straggling huts.

In this soft afterglow each leaf
Seems quivering with some sense of grief.

XV.   A GREEN WAVE.

Between the salt sea-send before
　　And all the flowing gulphs behind,
　　Half lifted by the rising wind,
Half eager for the ungain'd shore,
A great green wave of shining light
Sweeps onward crowned with dazzling white :

Above, the east wind shreds the sky
With plumes from the grey clouds that fly.

XVI.   MORNING GLORY.

Amber and gold and amethyst,
　　And carmine shot with crimson through,
　　And, quivering in the tender blue,
The fires of Phosphor o'er a mist
Of wild-rose pink—and overhead
The immaculate azure far outspread.

The unsubstantial hills loom fair
In delicate shadows thro' the air.

XVII. DAWN AMID SCOTCH FIRS.

The furtive lights that herald dawn
  Are shimmering 'mid the steel-blue firs ;
  A slow awakening wind half stirs
And the long branches breathes upon ;
The east grows clearer—clearer—lo,
The day is born ! A refluent flow

Of silver waves along each tree
For one brief moment dazzlingly.

XVIII. GROUND-LIGHTNING.

The mountain-range in purple looms
  From out the twilight-haunted west ;
  Star-crown'd, far east, Schehallion's crest
O'ertops the night ; here, where there booms
The bittern's hollow voicing harsh,
Gleam blue, green, yellow o'er the marsh

Strange furtive lights : the ghosts they seem
Of lightnings that shall no more stream.

XIX. THE EBBING TIDE.

A long low gurgle down the strand,
  The sputtering of the drying wrack !
  The tide is slowly ebbing back
With listless murmuring from the land,
And the small waves reluctant flow
Where the broad-bosomed currents go.

The sea has fall'n asleep, and lies
Dense blue beneath the dense blue skies.

XX. THE INCOMING TIDE.

Grey-glimmering thro' the dusky air
  The spectral cliffs loom o'er the sea,
  And up the strand tumultuously
The windy tidal billows tear :
How stern yon rock—nay, look once more,
The heedless waves above it pour !

Borne inwards o'er the spray-swept land
In thunder booms the sea's command.

XXI. TWO OLD YEWS.

Here 'neath the shade of cloisters vast
  Two immemorial yew-trees stand,
  Like pilgrims from an ancient land
Long long ago in the dim past
They saw the mystic Druid rites
Appease strange gods thro' bodeful nights.

Their boughs dead centuries enfold—
Deathless they seem, tho' scarred and old.

XXII. PHOSPHORESCENT SEA.

The sea scarce heaves in its calm sleep,
  The wind has not awakened yet
  Tho' in its dreams it seems to fret,
For, ever and again, the deep
Hearkens a sigh that steals along
As might some echo of sad song :

Ah, there the wind stirs ! Lo, the dark
Dim sea's on fire around our barque.

L.

XXIII.   PHOSPHORESCENT SEA.   (I.)   [II]

As when the face of one thought dead·
  Breaks into ghastly life again,
  The sea becomes a fiery plain
Of flames, blue, yellow, green, and red ;
Each wave seems some drown'd mariner
Upheaved from depths that no winds stir :

Surely the sea has long since died,
And now lies rotting, putrefied.*

XXIV.   PHOSPHORESCENT SEA.   (II.)   [III .]

How beautiful ! the violet waves
  Break upon orange-coloured seas ;
  And at each impulse of the breeze
A green and crimson ocean laves
The ship's black sides : as wild and strange
As those swift lights that burn and change

In glory ere the Polar morn
Dawns on the frozen wastes forlorn.

---

* A repetition of the metaphor in lines eleven and twelve of page
24, *The Human Inheritance.*

XXV. MOUNTAIN MISTS.

As though the bleak and lonely hill
   Were some drear desolate mount in hell
   Where spirits by some potent spell
Were forced to circle—damp and chill
The grey wan mists trail hour by hour
From crag to crag, and cling and cower.

From where the rain-cloud shrouds the peak
An eagle flings at times a shriek.

XXVI. MOONRISE *(August)*.

The wheat lies close in cluster'd gold
   Pale as the ore of Austral mines,
   For just above the tree-tops shines
The moon, full-orb'd : within the fold
The drowsy sheep seem fleeced with snow,
And branches, swaying to and fro

In the faint wind, in radiance gleam,
Each turn'd to silver by some beam.

XXVII. MOONRISE *(November).* *

The first snows of the year lie white
  Upon the branches bending low ;
  A surging wind the flakes doth blow
Before the coming feet of night—
Half dusk, half day, betwixt the pines
Green-yellow the full moon reclines :

Green-yellow, and now wholly green,
While faint the windy stars are seen.

XXVIII. MOONRISE *(December).*

The snow-clad fields are flushed with red,
  As though the sun's last dying rays
  Ensanguin'd them with crimson blaze—
For lo, in the wan skies o'erhead
The moon hangs as though dipped in blood :
And almost the stream's frozen flood

Seems like a wound that has just bled
Till now the earth lies cold and dead.

---

* The phenomenal aspects of the moon described in these and the
succeeding lines were observed by the writer during a winter stay of
some six or eight weeks amongst the mountain districts of Dumfries-
shire.

XXIX.—PINES IN STORM.

Hark ! like a wild and furious sea
  Where the bleak send and driving spray
  Harrow the dying face of day
A sound swells up tumultuously !
Amongst the pines the tempest dwells,
And swells and moans, and moans and swells.

Each pine, like some sad spirit, cries
Stricken and weary 'neath drear skies.

XXX.—THE LONELY LARCH.

Two cliffs stupendous frown upon
  The sunless pass far down below—
  Far down the hawks dart to and fro
Like flies within the twilight wan ;
And here, in the sun's sinking blaze
A lonely windy larch-tree sways :

Sole living thing at this great height
It is the wind's sport day and night.

THE TIDES OF VENICE.

ITH a soft slow gentle motion
Swings the slow tide from the sea,
Swings the slow tide hushfully
From the distant restless ocean,
Through the sinuous canals,
Past the ancient wave-worn walls
That have seen the galleys sweep
With great captain of the deep,
Fresh from where the Moslem calls
The Muezzin from the steep
Temple-domes that face the sea.
With a slow and gentle motion,
Like low breathing, ceaselessly
The tide steals from the ocean,
As a cloud that thro' the sky
Ever draweth, draweth nigh,
Though its white wings seem to beat
No wind that blows at all,

The Tides of Venice.

But lie folded calm and sweet
By its soft immaculate side—
So moves the sleeping tide
   Past bridge and palace wall.
And hung in purple heaven
   God's footstool fill'd with light
And wheel'd by spirits seven,
Seems the clear soul of night
So pure, so soft, so bright—
   The very soul it seems
   Of Venice of the deep
   Lying hush'd and still in sleep
'Neath the glory of her beams,
Dreaming, dreaming ancient dreams.
And like silver fires aglow
   The panting planets shine
And search the waters far below,
The waters that with stilly flow
     Come and go
   Beyond the salt sea line.
A faint wind is playing
   With the small sea-waves
   Above the myriad graves
O'er which move swaying, swaying
   The long green tangled reeds

And grasses of the sea,
And softly stir the slimy weeds
    That cling to where the salt sea laves
The stairs of palaces that be
No longer great or free.
At times, the shadows leaving,
    Black shapes leap forth and glide
    Like great fish on the tide—
    And singing side by side
The gondolieri, cleaving
    With lithe and rhythmic oar
The waters slowly heaving,
    Chant their old sea-born lore,
The old monotonous song
The tides have swept for long
    Round the Adriatic shore.
The very soul of mystery
    Seems brooding here alone :
    Each bridge and pier and stone
Holds secrets of the sea ;
The slow tide hushfully
    Moves with a scarce heard moan
And soft caressing motion,
    For their past to it is known,
To it and the silent ocean.

Hark! from yon window singing,
Slowly, gently, singing,
A woman with a perfect face
Dreams out into the night,
Her low voice, bird-like winging
Faint o'er the watery ways ;
Fashion'd with flawless grace,
Haloed with tender light,
She seems some angel pure and bright.
The sweet voice swelleth slowly
With music rich and deep ;
Sweeter than when in sleep
The soul with earth-closed eyes
In a vision holy
Hears the strains of Paradise :
And gaining volume still doth rise
Till all the wild notes sweep
In full majestic song
The dim canals along,
And like a fading memory then dies
I know that voice! 'Tis hers who came
To Venice with a singer's fame,]
A voice God gave her as a sign
He gives sometimes what is divine,
A face for Dolorous Mary's shrine

All loveliness the tongue can name,
A mind impervious to shame
 And spirit of a concubine.
The gondolieri, as they pass
 Her palace, mark it with a laugh :
 The gamesters turn and quaff
Their wine to her whose heart of dust
Claims kinship with their own coarse lust.
 So fair, so seeming holy,
As wrapt in some pure dream
Where heaven more near doth seem,
 While the salt-tides ebb, ebb slowly
  With murmurs melancholy
 O harlot ! is thy breath
 But some sweet mask of death ?
If this thy last great song should be
 What shall come unto the,
 Poor wreckage of life's sea !
O Venice, art thou such an one,
 Thou who hast been
 Crown'd as a queen
Amidst the nations !   Hast thou won
The saffron robes that mark the lost,
 Thou whom the blue waves tossed
Around, when all thy flags unfurl'd

Waved defiance to the world ;
Whom the fierce Turk strove in vain
To vanquish ; who hast hurl'd
Thine omnipotence against the might of Spain,
    Thou nursling of the wind
    And playmate of the sea—
O ! is the loveliness we find
    Still clinging unto thee
        A bitter mockery ?
Art thou too dead and lonely,
    Like her who ruled of old,—
    Tyre, crown'd with ancient gold ?
Or, art thou sleeping only
        To wake some distant day,
To shake thy sea-blown hair again,
To snap thy rusted chain,
    To see the world behold
        The glory of thy sway ?
    O city of the sea
    Laved by the salt sea-tides
    That daily ebb and flow
    With long wash ceaselessly
Around thy wave-worn sides,
Thou art as she who sang
    With angel voice and heart of dust !

Thou too art cast aside of men,
Thy war-cries long since rang
   Their last fierce clang,
Thou also art the sport of lust,
As mighty Tyre was, when
   Her glory was a thing
   To jeer at, and the owlet's wing
Haunted her palace walls,
So shalt thou, Venice, be
   When all thy great canals,
   What all thy lords possess
   And thine own loveliness
Are levelled with the sea
Slow, with a steadfast motion,
   The salt-tides ebb away
   Sweep hushfully away
Towards the silent ocean :
Ere long the sea-line grey
   Far east will shake with gold,
   And Venice, weary and old,
Will see another day
   Make all her beauty fair
   In the blue enfolding air.
Meanwhile past bridge and palace,
   Past each carv'd wave-worn stone,

'With low incessant moan
The tide flows forth alone
.Its burdens to efface,
To whisper the disgrace
  And all the shame and woe
  To the sea where it doth flow.
.O tides of life that wander
  Led by some unseen hand
  About our mortal strand,
As the salt sea-tides yonder
  Ye, in your ebb and flow,
  Gather our joy and woe ;
And in your swift retreating
  Surge joy and exaltation,
  The wails of desolation/
'Great hopes in strong hearts beating
  Tears, laughter, prayers, and pain.:
  But ever back again
These come with ceaseless iteration.
O that your floods could bear
  To some unmeasured sea
  The long dull agony,
'Grief, sorrow, anguish, care,
  Shall fill men evermore,
  Far from our human shore ;

And bearing so could bring
  When in your earthward flow
  Instead of further woe
To each some fair sweet thing—
    Some hope fulfill'd, some new desire,
        Some rest for weary feet,
    A spark of the immortal fire
    Wherewith mankind can still aspire
    To something nobler, grander, higher,
        Some joy sad eyes to meet
        Some message sweet.
Hush! with what gentle swaying
  The twilight waters go
  As seaward still they flow ;
A new-born wind is playing
  And singing weird strange runes
  Out on the grey lagunes ;
And tolling to and fro,
With a music sad and slow,
  A convent bell is ringing
  O'er the cowled monks bent and singing—
Through the sinuous canals,
Past the ancient wave-worn walls
With a soft slow gentle motion
    Swings the ebb-tide to the sea,
    Swings the slow tide hushfully
To the distant restless ocean.

A DIALOGUE.

Nature.

Lo here, in this calm sea where no waves whirl,
I make some thought renascent in this pearl—
Must it remain and know no nobler sphere
Than twilight waters ever calm and clear ?

God.

Deep in calm seas quiescent let it lie :
Its pure perfection none shall e'er descry
Save the omniscient omnipresent eye
That loves the secrets of the earth and sky.

Nature.

Beneath this vast and craggy peak there dwells
Long lullabied by subterranean wells
Of icy waters dark as darkest night,
A gem of wonderful translucent light :

Shall it remain unguessed, unsought, alone,
A living heart in this eternal stone?

God.

Nay, let some miner in the mountain's womb
Come on this ruby gleaming thro' the gloom :
Its place sufficeth not, it hath no room
To send forth rays, it seeks a nobler doom—
Yea, let it go, and feel a woman's breath,
And be the bale-star of a shattered faith
And lead a dying nation to its death.

Nature.

Lo, on strewn palm-leaves in this unknown isle
A new-born babe upon the world doth smile :
The mystic essence shines from out his eyes,
Pure as the angels without spot or guile—
Shall its soul now, while pure regain the skies?

God.

Nay, let it know the wild free joyous bliss
Of morn and eve, of heedless winds that kiss
The dewy lips of flowers while still they sleep,
Of singing birds, and beasts that run and leap,—

Let him live out his life without a thought,
A perfect animal, the soul forgot,
Until the cycle of his years doth creep
Closer and wrap both body and soul in sleep.

Nature.

Behold, within yon far off teeming town
A woman thanks thee for her life's chief crown,
A child is hers, whom all fair hopes surround :
Shall he not live and make his age resound
With wisdom long sought after, seldom found ?

God.

Let his unswathed soul come forth to me
A spirit upon earth it shall not be.
I call for one to come and one to stay ;
For this to shine far from the light of day,
And this to dazzle eyes of men away ;
One shall return again to primal force,
Another shall attain an infinite course—
Yet all are as the same to me who know
The ultimate ebb of things and the first flow.

M

DESOLATION.

I COME from dark and tempest
    From lands that know ño peace,
From mansions where ño stray guest
  Of travail hath surcease,
Where grey wan skies of morning
    Slow fade to ~~slower~~ eve,
And echoing winds of scorning
    Subside in sobs that grieve.

I stand alone and lonely,
    And watch each dark day die ;
Night breaks again and only
    More desolate grows the sky :
And while my heart grows faint then
    With all its weary lot
The phantom shades of dead men
    (To me dead) know me not.

I see the long years creeping
   That have not come to me,
The days thereof all weeping
   With sad eyes bitterly,
And oh I know each morrow
   That thrills with anguish low
Hath a deeper sense of sorrow,
   Is crown'd with weighter woe.

CHRISTMAS-EVE.

ONE eve, when the cold snow lay white
      Along the silent street,
   A little child, all clothed in light
And with a smile most sweet,

Did enter my dim lonely room
   As chimed the midnight bell :—
" I am thy Life, thy Death, thy Doom,
   For thee I entered Hell !"

" O little child," I said, "art thou
   Some messenger divine ?"
He pointed to his tender brow
   Round which soft light did shine,

And there I saw a shadowy crown,
   Of plaited thorns 'twas wrought,
And from each thorn there trickled down
   A liquid crimson spot.

And while I looked he faded slow
   And vanish'd from my sight:
Only the gusty wind did blow
   The wild snow through the night.

And when in after-dreams I lay
   I heard the white hosts cry
" Hosanna ! on this day
   The Christ comes from on high !"

LIFE.

 " SWEET, sweet, sweet
        Is life," a bird sang loud ;
        And underneath a crowd
Listened with weary wayworn feet.
" How sweet,
O sweet, sweet, sweet ! "

" O sad, sad, sad
Is life," a bird thrilled loud ;
And underneath, a crowd
Moaned also, with torn bleeding feet,
" How sad,
O sad, sad, sad ! "

SIGHT.

 **I** LOOKED in the eyes of a brute,
    I looked on the face of a man,
    A blossom, a flower, a fruit,
An insect, all links of a plan :
I gazed thro' the depths of the sea,
    On clouds, and on mountains afar ;
And I saw the chain twine around me
    And reach to the farthest star.

YOUNG LOVE.

ON a flower in a forest,
    A lily-bosom'd flower,
    (Where never windy tempest
Came, nor ever any shower)—
A golden hour of birthtide,
    (The sky was blue, so blue!)
Left me lying 'mid a songtide
    Of birds of every hue.

Upon the white flower swaying
    I laughed and sang in glee,
Till the thrushes long delaying
    Sang back deliciously;
And the clear white cloudlets sleeping
    Up in the blue, blue sky,
Seem'd downy cherubs peeping
    Between the pine boughs high.

A little wind came blowing
　And sang a wild-wood song,
It whispered of the flowing
　Of bubbling streams along ;
I laughed, and stood, and rising
　Found I had two small wings—
So then I flew rejoicing
　Towards the water-springs.

And ever 'mid my flying,
　(A little cloud I seem'd !)
I heard a great deep sighing,
　As earth in trouble dream'd ;
And when I reached the river
　The sound more windlike blew :—
The glad stream lisped "*for ever*,"—
　But the sighing grew and grew.

And as I laughed and wonder'd
　Among the flow'rs and grass,
All suddenly it thunder'd,
　The sunlight seem'd to pass :

A great wind took and blew me
Across a grey wet sand,
And tho' I wept it threw me
Far from the joyous land.

And now the salt waves leaping
Pursue with hungry springs,
And baffled, blind, and weeping,
I beat my draggled wings :
This was the great deep sighing
I heard when I was young—
And now, wind-weary, dying,
My last sob-note is sung !

DREAM LAND.

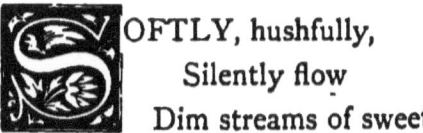OFTLY, hushfully,
Silently flow
Dim streams of sweetness
Thro' lands of woe ;
Hushfully, hushfully
Wash the cool waves
Thro' intricate spaces
Of sea-worn caves ;
And silently, suddenly
Gather wan faces
Long laid in graves.

Speechless, and yearning
O with sad eyes !
And wan hearts burning
With memories :
Silently, silently,

Gath'ring around
From cool dark places
  Of churchyard ground :
O the wan faces
  Whose lips have no sound.

Hushfully, hushfully,
  Strange rivers flow
Thro' silent lands
  No soul doth know ;
Peacefully, peacefully,
  Restful and slow,
Faint music of wings
  On the tired wind doth go ;
Hushfully, hushfully,
  Hushfully so
Whether with pleasure
  Or woe.

A GREETING.

(*TO E. L. H.*)

HE month, in whose warm heart is graven
    deep
    The cuckoo's farewell voice, waits behind
    May,
Her frolic sister, who upon the way
Strews blossoms laughing : from their long dark sleep
Daily the blessèd roses stir and creep
    From fold and bud : and thro' the twilight grey
    That dreams about the haunts of vanish'd day
The culver calleth from the wooded steep.

I, in the busy haunts of men, but dream
    Of these, as thou upon thy weary bed :
Yet every day we know the blue skies gleam
    And ev'ry night the star-lamps shine, o'erhead—
Is it not well with us that we can feel
At least such memoried raptures o'er us steal ?

REVELATION.

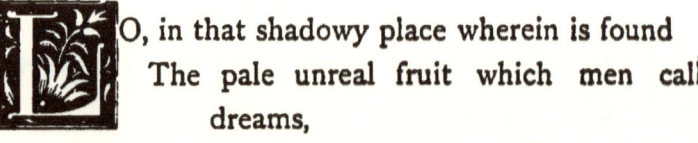O, in that shadowy place wherein is found
 The pale unreal fruit which men call
 dreams,
I wander'd. Ever underneath wan gleams
Of misty moonlight faintly shining round—
Long resting on the silent trees as sound
 Before awakening, and o'er sedgy streams
 Moving like wind in broad and quivering beams—
A spirit walked beside me. From a mound,
Rustling with poplar leaves from top to base,
 Some bird I knew not shrilled a cry of dole,
So bitter, I cried out to God for grace :
 Then spake that one, *While onward thy years roll*
Thou shalt be haunted by this hated face—
 And looking up I looked on mine own soul.

POSSIBILITIES.

S day doth live beyond the sunset skies
So life may wait us at the silent grave :
Not windless is the sea because there rave
Not always the great storm-wind's harmonies.
There may be light too strong for earthly eyes ;
There may be hands to succour and to save
From Death's indifferent o'erwhelming wave ;
Nay, Death may lift to some divine surprise!

There may be music beyond instruments
And Spring for ev'ry frost night shapeless clad,
There may be mightier love sacraments
Than e'er were seen on consecrated sod ;
A man there may be with Christ's lineaments
And mid the wheels of Fate a living God!

PAIN.

 AM God's eldest :—I and Love are twin ;
We look for ever in the other's face ;
Together our flight wings throughout all
    space—
Sun, Star, Man, God, alike we dwell therein ;
Some far-off goal together strive to win.
   But here on earth I leave the mightier trace,
   Clasp hands more close with all the human race,
And weave the shadow-webs of joy and sin.
And most I dwell in the clear skies at dawn,
   In marvellous eves when all the stars are bright,
In music e'er the sweetest chord is gone,
   In woman's beauty still unsoiled and white,
In children's slumber in the morning wan,
   And lover's vows and yearnings in the night.

BEN-A-CHAOLAIS (*The Mountain of Sounds*).*

HE wild Atlantic blasts whirl day and night
    Their rheum upon it, and the mountain
        stands
Frowning immoveably, as a giant with bands
Chained to the ground' beholds the insulting light.
Hark! are they sea-mews in their wailing flight
These dismal echoes moaning o'er the sands?
Or swell the cries from weird unearthly lands
Borne' hence upon the wild wind's wings of might?

Thou art the image of a human soul,
    O lonely hill, fronting the blasts of fate—
    Like thee for ever haunted by wild cries
From secret depths, and heedless of the roll
    Of whirling seas with deathful strength elate,
    Or the long desolate darkness of the skies.

---

* One of the Paps of Jura overlooking the Atlantic. It is honey-combed in its seaward front with hollow narrow caverns running often far inland, where strange currents of air and echoing tidal billows are ever moving: hence, both in calm and tempest, strange wailing sounds seem to issue from its depths.

N

SPRING-WIND.

FULL-VOICED herald of immaculate
   spring,   *Cap*
With clarion gladness striking every tree
   To answering raptures, as a resonant sea
   Fills rock-bound shores with thunders echoing—
O thou, each beat of whose tempestuous wing
   Shakes the long winter-sleep from hill and lea,
   And rouses with loud reckless jubilant glee
   The birds that have not dared as yet to sing :

O wind, that comest with prophetic cries,
   Hast thou indeed beheld the face that is
   The joy of poets and the glory of birds—
Spring's face itself : hast thou 'neath bluer skies
Met the warm lips that are the gates of bliss,
   And heard June's leaf-like murmur of sweet words ?

Reprinted from Mr. T. Hall Caine's *Three Centuries*
English Sonnets. (Elliot Stock : 1882.)

TO THE SPIRIT CALLED LAUDANUM.

ALMER of pain that would be agony,
   O spirit, who with hands benign doth
   keep
The tired soul shrouded in a veil of sleep,—
Who silently takes up the last faint sigh
As angel souls of children when they die—
   Whose breath is as those waves upon the deep
   Born in a tempest but who softly creep
Towards windless calms where motionless they lie.

I feel the silence brooding from thy gaze,
   I see the shadow of thy slumberous wing
      Shroud the slow ebb of pain's reluctant tide—
O spirit, whose feet haunt the silent ways
   Of sleep and death where voices never ring,
      I hear the sea where all tired waves subside.

LINES.

to *F . A . S .*

AIR in my sight as white lilies that shine in
   the sunrise:
Sweeter than flow'rs in the meadows that
   scent the mornings of spring :
Dearer than vision of truth, for thou art the truth
   revealéd,
Dearer than faith, for thou art the crown of aspiration,
Dearer than hope, for of hope thou art the fulfilment !
O love, love, love, thou hast turned the darkness of
   the world
Into ineffable light, and all its intricate ways
To straight, clear paths that lead from the depths to
   the heavens.
The flow'r of my soul sways high in the wind of thy
   love,
Glowing with passionate fervour through fulness of
   joy ;
Soul with soul are we wedded, beyond the decay of
   the body,

And spirit hath spirit touched, beyond the confines of
flesh :
Desire with mighty wings/hath swept the chords of
our being,   .
And flesh and spirit are one in the mystic union of
love !

---

* These lines, and those following, entitled *The Redeemer*, must
not be judged as hexametrical efforts.   They were portion of a series
written similarly irregularly, when the author held rather heretical
views on the limitations of the sonnet and on verse-structure
generally.   They are inserted simply for the truth that, to the
writer, is set forth in each.

THE REDEEMER.

 KNOW that my Redeemer liveth—but out
of the depths of time
He hath not called to me yet.   But from
th' immeasurable tracts
That widen unending to where beginneth eternity
Falleth at times a voice, heart-thrilling, soul-piercing,
life-giving ;
High sometimes and clear, as a lark singing in a holy
dawn,
Hush'd and afar off again as a dreaming wave upon
seas
Lit by a low vast moon, and windlessly sleeping, but
ever
Sweet with a human love, and full of ineffable
yearning,
And crying of soul unto soul from infinite deep unto
deep.
And sometimes I look and gaze out upon uttermost
darkness

And hear the wail of desolate winds moaning around
the world—

Till the darkness shivers to light, and clashing thro'
earth and heaven

I hear great wings make music, and marvellous
thunderous songs

Shout "thy Redeemer liveth," O human soul and
crieth for thee!

LAST WORDS.

(To the one who has always first read everything I have written.)

OW can I tell thee, dear, what never words
Have fitly told? How hope my heart to thee
Wherein thou might'st, as in a well, perceive
Deep down but the mere shadow of my love?
But as the wind sweeps from the icy north
To some lov'd isle in dim pacific seas,
Or as the never-ceasing circling waves
Follow round earth the radiant orb of night,
So follow I with love unspeakable
The pathways fill'd with light which are thine own.
O love, thou art the flame that burns for me,
My steady purpose! That no dark can quench!
Holding thy hand I fear no more to watch
The shifting of the changeful lights of Fate.